SOLE SURVIVOR

Also by
Ruthanne Lum McCunn

Thousand Pieces of Gold

SOLE SURVIVOR

Ruthanne Lum McCunn

Beacon Press
Boston

Beacon Press
25 Beacon Street
Boston, Massachusetts 02108-2892
www.beacon.org

Beacon Press books
are published under the auspices of
the Unitarian Universalist Association of Congregations.

First Beacon Press edition published in 1999

Printed in the United States of America

04 03 02 01 00 99 8 7 6 5 4 3 2 1

This book is printed on recycled acid-free paper that contains at least
20 percent postconsumer waste and meets the uncoated paper
ANSI/NISO specifications for permanence as
revised in 1992.

Library of Congress Cataloging-in-Publication Data

McCunn, Ruthanne Lum.
Sole survivor : a story of record endurance at sea / Ruthanne Lum
McCunn.
p. cm.
ISBN 0-8070-7139-0 (paper)
1. Poon, Lim—Fiction. 2. Survival after airplane accidents,
shiprecks, etc.—Fiction. 3. World War, 1939–1945—Fiction.
I. Title.
PS3563.C353S6 1999
813'.54—dc21 99–14163

In Memory of
my father, Captain Robert Drake Drysdale,
who loved the sea.

And for those,
living and dead, who contributed in no small
measure to my survival during my first years
in America, especially Captain Gus Landberg,
Sandy Adams Hilliard, Lynda D. Preston,
Georgie Blake, Janina and Stanislaw Slawik,
and Evelyn, Jim, and Alison Hulse.

ACKNOWLEDGMENTS

I am grateful to Poon Lim for sharing his story with me. Without his cooperation, the research for this book would have been far more difficult. I also wish to thank his family for sharing their recollections. Poon Mei Mui's vivid descriptions of village life and Poon Gee Han's detailed family history were especially valuable in reconstructing Mr. Poon's childhood in Hainan.

I am indebted to Samuel Harby for taking the time to answer my questions, his encouragement and suggestions when I hit apparent dead ends, and his careful reading of my manuscript for accuracy.

I am also grateful to John Yee and the Chinese Historical Society of Southern California for sharing the tapes of their interview with Mr. Poon, and Margie Lew for first providing inspiration and then critically reading my final draft.

It would be impossible to name all the other people who generously shared their expertise with me during the different stages of this project. However, I would like to thank the following persons in particular: Keith Welsh, Hong Kong Manager for The Ben Line; Alec M. Peill, Group Public Relations, The Ben Line Steamers Ltd., Scotland; P.R. Melton, Naval Historical Branch, Ministry of Defence, London; Nicola Smith, Guildhall Library, London; J.E. Headspeath, Dept. of Nautical Catering, Colquitt Technical & Nautical Catering College, Liverpool; Jean Hood, Information Officer, Lloyd's Register of Shipping, London; Simon Stephens, Dept. of Ships, National Maritime Museum, Greenwich, London; Harry E. Rilley, Modern Military Headquarters Branch, Military Archives Division, Washington D.C.; B.F. Cavalcante, Operational Archives, Dept. of the Navy, Naval Historical Center, Washington D.C.; Elaine C. Everly, Assistant Chief, Navy & Old Army Branch,

Military Archives Division, Washington D.C.; Dr. Steven Webster, Director of Education, Monterey Bay Aquarium; Charles Burdick, Dean, School of Social Sciences, San Jose State University; Catherine Brady, Rita Drysdale, Captain Robert E. Durkin, Elise Earthman, Mary Lou Harby, Marlon Hom, Steven Kahn, Hoi Lee, Drummond McCunn, Jay Schaeffer, Judy Susman, John Kuo Wei Tchen, Jan & Wayne Venolia, Ellen Lai-shan Yeung, and Judy Yung. Their diverse contributions were crucial to the final shape of this book.

I also wish to acknowledge the assistance of the librarians at the California Maritime Academy, the National Archives, the San Francisco Public Library, the libraries of the University of California at Berkeley, and the Hong Kong Urban Council Library at City Hall; and the staff and volunteers of the National Liberty Ship Memorial in San Francisco.

But my greatest debts are to my sister, Robin Grossman, and my husband, Donald McCunn, for their special insights and unflagging support during the last three years; and to my friend, Lynda Preston, for her editorial guidance.

PROLOGUE

Less than twelve hours after war was declared in 1939, a German U-boat torpedoed the British passenger liner *Athenia* without warning. "Sink at sight" continued to be Germany's policy. Within two months, fifty-six Allied and neutral merchant ships had been sunk by mines and U-boats, and thousands of non-combatants killed or drowned.

Increasingly high casualties and the growth of war-associated shipping created a need for additional man-power, and in 1940 the British Merchant Navy sent out a call for Chinese seamen. Poon Lim was among those who answered the call. A young man of twenty-two, he signed articles of agreement for Second Steward on the *Benlomond*—a Scots-officered ship of 9,675 tons, with a crew of forty-seven (half Scots and half Chinese) and eight gunners.

British merchant ships, under government control, traded when and where required by the Allies, taking arms to forces overseas, then bringing back food and raw materials to England. Because merchant ships were only lightly armed, any confrontations with U-boats or cruisers were one-sided. Convoys offered only limited protection since the U-boats were faster than many of the escorts, and one-third of the ships sunk were those in convoy.

Even in port, a ship was not always safe. The *Benlomond*, while loading explosives in Holehaven, England, barely avoided a floating mine. And when the sheds alongside her took fire during an air raid, she had to be moved to a safer position on the other side of the dock by the sheer force of men pulling on ropes and hawsers.

The biggest danger, however, was the middle part of the Atlantic run where no air cover was possible. There, wolf packs of U-boats concentrated their attacks, and in the first seven months of 1942, 681 ships weighing a total of 3-1/2 million tons were sunk. Hitler claimed the Allies had yet to feel the full might of his submarine blitz, and he promised that any sailor foolish enough to sail would stand little chance of returning.

Nevertheless, Poon Lim, like other men, continued to sign new articles, and when the *Benlomond* left Capetown, in ballast, on November 10, 1942, to pick up cargo in Paramaribo, Dutch Guiana, Poon Lim sailed with her. Thirteen days later, in position 00.30 N, 38.45 W, 750 miles east of the Amazon River, she was sunk by two torpedoes. All hands were lost, except Poon Lim.

This is his story.

CHAPTER ONE

In his quarters high above the *Benlomond's* engine room, Lim lay on his bunk, one leg braced against a rib in the bulkhead. The *Benlomond*, though very light and high, rode the sea well. But the precautionary zig-zag meant the ship swung from starboard to port and back every twenty minutes, and she leaned sharply with each turn. Though he could not see or hear them, Lim could sense men all over the ship preparing for a change of watch. The engineers' steward with whom he shared the cabin had gone below already, but Lim lingered, rolling and lighting another cigarette. He puffed nervously.

In the six years since he first shipped out, he had risen from learn boy to Second Steward. But he knew no more about ships and the sea now than he did then. Not because he did not want to learn. He did. Taking hot tea and cocoa to officers on the bridge, he became fascinated by the instruments; and he asked to learn how to trace currents, to read wind and waves, to chart a course with sun and stars — all the skills necessary to match wits with the ocean. But it was forbidden. Chinese worked as stewards, cooks, donkeymen, firemen, and painters. Not mates.

Determined to learn a trade, he quit the sea after three years and enrolled in the Wah Nam Mechanics School in Hong Kong. Though he did not understand the teachers' Cantonese dialect, he enjoyed working with his hands, puzzling out solutions for problem engines and devising replacements for broken parts. But after only six months, a cousin who was Chief Steward on the *Benlomond* warned Lim that the Japanese would soon invade Hong Kong and advised him to leave while he still had a chance. So he signed on under his cousin as Second Steward.

As Lim's cousin had predicted, Hong Kong fell to the Japanese, so Lim could not regret his decision to return to sea. But the constant threat of a sinking was a strain from which there was no escape except for a few hours ashore once every three or four weeks. Even then, air raids and the mines laid around many of the ports spoiled any chance for true relaxation. But the older hands promised that Paramaribo, which they should reach in another six days, would be different, less touched by war.

Lim glanced at his watch. 11:40. If he didn't hurry, he would be late reporting to serve tiffin. Taking one last drag on the cigarette, he ground it out in the ashtray wedged between the bulkhead and himself, and swung down onto the deck. Swiftly he dusted off the bits of ash and tobacco clinging to his singlet, pulled a mess jacket over it, knotted the waistband of his loose Chinese trousers, stepped into his slippers, and ran his fingers through his thick black hair.

The ship lurched, slamming him across the engineer steward's bunk; then she heeled sharply, flinging him onto the deck. Ashtray, bedding, and mattress tumbled after him, and he heard a great creaking and thrashing of gear. Staggering to his feet, he wondered if a lookout had sighted a submarine. An explosion rocked through the tiers of steel decks, hurling Lim back onto the deck. He stared, stunned, as a pillar of water shot past the shattered porthole. The ship shuddered. He heard muffled cries, the sound of stores torn loose skidding across decks, a steady hissing. Then a second explosion, fiercer than the first, catapulted him into the alley, and he realized that the *Benlomond* had been torpedoed.

Weekly drills made his actions automatic, and he scrambled back into the cabin to grab his life jacket. He found it in a tangle of bedding and gear, yanked it free, and stumbled down the alley. Gusts of hot, acrid smoke billowed out of the ventilators. Shielding his nose and mouth with his life jacket, he struggled to keep his footing as the ship began to list, right itself, then list again, hurling him against bulkheads, fleeing men, the ladder to the boat deck.

The ship was pitched too steeply for him to climb the ladder to his assigned boat station without both hands, so he stopped and pulled on his life jacket, taking precious seconds to fasten the straps and ties while others pushed past shouting at him to hurry. Finally, his hands freed, he pulled himself up by the railing.

The air on the boat deck was black with smoke. But there was no mistaking the empty space between the chocks, the falls swinging slack from the davits: The lifeboat was gone.

Fighting panic, Lim leaned, coughing, against the rail. Below him, scalding steam hissed out of the smashed engine room skylight, and he could hear the screams of trapped firemen. A wall of dull orange fire crackled around the air-exhaust shields, creeping over the oil that was spilling out of ruptured pipes. Small knots of men slid across buckled decks, tripping over loosened rivets and sheared plates. An officer slashed the lanyards lashing the rafts to the forward mast, cursed as they skittered clumsily into piles of loose debris.

Stinking black oil oozed into the sea through gaping holes in the hull, and the grind of twisting metal rose above the sound of engines barely turning over. The ship was still making headway, but she was settling ominously, and the sea was breaking over the deck amidships.

Suddenly, the ship listed sharply, breaking Lim's grip on the rail. Steadying himself, he caught a glimpse of a seaman and the Second and Third Mates struggling to launch the lifeboat at the bridge station, and he scrambled over to help them.

As a steward, Lim had been through hundreds of drills without once actually lowering a boat. Now his inexperience, his inability to understand the officers' orders, and the canted deck made him clumsy. Then, just as they raised the boat off the chocks, a noise like thunder ripped through the *Benlomond's* bowels.

"The bulkhead of the main hold's collapsed. Tie your life jackets on tight and go over the side," the Second Mate ordered.

Without a moment's hesitation, the seaman and the Third Mate jumped. As their bodies disappeared beneath green black water, the Second Mate pushed Lim towards the rail. "For God's sake, jump! Then swim like mad or you'll be sucked down with the ship," he shouted, pantomiming how Lim should hold his nose with one hand, hug his life jacket with the other, then jump and swim.

Before Lim could respond, the stern plummeted. Tons of green sea poured into the ship, forcing it into a death roll, and Lim was sucked into a punishing black swirl. Tortured water dragged him down, popping his ears, ripping off his slippers, tearing loose his trousers. He fought to kick them free, but the whirling funnel bound him too tightly, and he spun deeper and deeper into the whirlpool boiling up from the *Benlomond's* violent plunge to her grave.

The pressure against his ears became unbearable. His lungs felt as if they would explode. If he could only ease the pressure a little, then he could hang on, he was sure. But instead of opening a crack, his mouth burst wide, and his lungs expelled the air they had held so long in an explosion of bubbles that danced, mocking, before his face. He bolted down a rush of water, gritted his teeth against more. But again his lips could not, would not hold, and he was sucking in great gulps of water and oil when, suddenly, he was propelled up, thrown from the sea as brutally as he had been swallowed.

Though he was spitting, coughing, and vomiting sea water and oil, the buoyancy of the kapok jacket that had brought Lim to the surface kept him afloat. But he needed something to hang on to, to steady him while he rubbed off the muck sealing his eyes and nose. Floating wreckage bumped against him. He grabbed wildly, caught hold of a broken board and dragged it close. Hugging it tightly with one arm, he cleared his nostrils as much as possible. Then he rubbed at the sticky ooze that blinded him. But his fingers, equally slimy, only made his eyes smart more. He scraped his palms and fingers against the coarse fabric of his life jacket. Slowly, jerkily, he worked open his sealed lids.

What he saw made him want to clamp them shut again. All that was left of the *Benlomond* was one or two large bubbles and a few wisps of smoke in a vast, evil-smelling pool of fuel oil. A broken spar. Shell cases. Bits and pieces of debris. The litter of fifty-five men. Men who now dangled from life jackets like dislocated puppets, bloody, charred, split open like broken gourds.

But if he was alive, there had to be others. The two officers and the seaman at the bridge station perhaps. Or the officer who had cut loose the rafts. The men who had taken the lifeboat from his assigned station. Those whose cries of pain rose above the slap of water against debris.

"Here, over here, I'm alive too," Lim yelled, first in Chinese and then in English.

Someone shouted, but he could not distinguish the words. Neither could he see where the sound was coming from, for the piece of wood he hugged and the glare of sun on oil restricted his vision to the area immediately around him, and his trousers shackled his legs so he could not move.

He tore at the trousers knotted around his ankles, ripping them free. Then, still clinging to the broken board, he kicked furiously, pushing out in one direction and then another, until finally he saw two men on a raft about 100 yards distant pulling a third on board.

"Here! Over here!" Lim called.

Trying awkwardly to maneuver the raft towards another man floundering just out of reach, the men gave no indication they saw or heard him.

Lim jerked the plank up and down, splashing, waving, and shouting.

Still they did not respond.

He was wasting his strength. Yet he could not stop. He had not swum since he was a boy on Hainan Island, and even then it had only been a childish dog paddle in the village stream where he could always reach his toes down to pebble-strewn sand for reassurance. That was why he had hesitated when the Second Mate ordered him to jump. That moment of hesitation had almost cost him his life, might rob him of it now, for the raft was drifting, the distance between him and the men growing wider as he clung to the false security of a broken board.

Deliberately, Lim pushed the piece of wood aside and struck out in a brave flail of arms and legs. His life jacket kept him afloat. But the thick blanket of oil that smoothed the swells also weighed down his limbs, and each time he looked up, the raft seemed farther away.

He tried calling out again, but his voice sounded thin and small even to his own ears, and a strange swell sloshed oil and salt water into his open mouth, choking him. Part of a hatch cover floated near, and he made a lunge for it. Fingers clawed splintered wood, got a proper grip, and he clung to the sturdy plank, panting and coughing.

The swells intensified and the long, narrow shaft of a periscope appeared dead ahead. Remembering talk of U-boats ruthlessly machine gunning survivors, Lim shrank down behind the plank as the periscope raked the horizon. It dipped a little, and for a moment he thought the submarine would submerge. Instead, there was a mighty convulsion, and a conning tower burst out of a swirl of scummy foam.

Almost immediately a hatch rasped open and a half dozen swarthy, bearded sailors scrambled out of the conning tower, spilled down the ladder, and spread across the grease-streaked hull to the gun decks fore and aft. One man remained on the bridge at the top of the conning tower. He shouted something down to those still in the submarine, and the stern of the submarine swept around and ground to a halt a few yards away from the raft which was rocking so crazily that the men on board were pinned flat on the deck.

The man on the bridge snapped another command, and the men at the guns trained them on the raft while two sailors, grappling with long boat hooks and rope, pulled it alongside. They tied it fast, then prodded the remnants of the *Benlomond's* crew on board, up the ladder to the conning tower, and into the submarine. Peering out from behind the broken hatch cover, Lim counted five men. But bobbing up and down and squinting against the glare, he could not be sure.

The man who had been giving the orders followed them below and the gunners and sailors relaxed. Lim watched enviously as one lit a cigarette and offered it to the aft gunner, then lit another. The other men lit up also, and they chatted, calling back and forth with easy camaraderie.

The sun beat down, baking Lim's head and neck, burning his scalp, the patches of skin free from grease. Below the surface, he felt a strange disembodied chill though the water was not cold. His mess jacket and singlet, twisted into uncomfortable creases beneath his life jacket, chafed. His throat ached for the taste of a cigarette. His head throbbed.

Were his cousin and cabinmate among those men on the raft? Were they now being interrogated? Or were they having smokes, something to eat? Would they be kept as prisoners of war or would they be released or shot? Should he call out or remain silent?

Nazis were supposed to be heartless, ordered by Hitler to kill the crews of the ships they sank. But the men laughing and chatting on the hull didn't seem ruthless.... Still shielding himself with the broken hatchcover, he examined the submarine more carefully. The hull was painted a pale gray, almost white, and the conning tower had an insignia. Only part of it was on the side facing Lim, but he could make out two colors, green and white....

Impulsively Lim pulled himself up high on the hatch cover, exposing his head and shoulders, and shouted, "Help! Over here! Help!"

Splashing water with both arms and the plank, he called out again and again. But his voice could not rise above the hum of idling engines, the bang of debris against the hull. He would have to try to swim the fifty yards to the submarine.

Pushing the hatch cover in front of him, he kicked strongly. The solid layer of oil that had slowed his progress before had been broken up by the submarine when it surfaced, and he plowed forward, creating a noisy, foamy trail. Before long, the aft gunner noticed him. He nudged the sailor beside him, and they beckoned, smiling. Encouraged, Lim's legs churned faster.

He had covered a little over half the distance when he saw the men from the *Benlomond* herded back onto the raft. With a grinding that sounded like the working of millstones, the submarine roared into life, throwing up great waves of plowed water that flung him backwards and wrenched the hatch cover from his arms.

"Help!" he gasped.

The sailors laughed, shaking their arms and legs in imitation of Lim.

"Save me or I drown," he cried.

Laughing even harder, the aft gunner leaned over his gun. He aimed it at Lim, pretending to fire as the submarine screamed past. Tossing helplessly in its wake, Lim saw the submarine turn in a great arc. The sailors vanished down hatches. He heard the clang of watertight doors, a rush of ominous gurgles. Then the submarine was sinking, and he was squeezing his eyes shut, steeling himself against the terrible sucking rush that had drawn him down with the *Benlomond.*

It did not happen.

There was very little turbulence.

There was no suction.

Yet when he opened his eyes, the submarine was gone. The raft also.

Had the submarine mowed it down, killing the men on board? Or were the men alive, hanging onto the few bits of wreckage still scattered about?

"Anyone there?" Lim called.

The only answer was an eerie silence.

An awful loneliness swept over Lim. And fear. And then a dogged determination. The *Benlomond* had carried two lifeboats and four rafts. He would swim until he found one of them.

His attempts to reach the raft and the submarine had weakened Lim, and he propelled his weary arms and legs forward in shallow little chops that quickly became smaller, weaker, and ever more shallow. He rolled over on his back, permitting his arms to rest while his legs continued kicking just hard enough to keep him moving. Then, when they refused to obey, he turned on his side, allowing his legs and one arm to rest while the other paddled.

Changing sides as often as his body demanded, he scoured the water for a lifeboat, a raft, another survivor, the terrifying triangle of a shark's fin. The sea was not rough, but each swell stretched a forbidding three to four feet from the bottom of a trough to its crest. Heaved high on an upward roll, he could see barren hills of water stretching to the horizon. Plunged into a watery valley, he was overcome with the feeling that he was being drawn into the sea....

Two hours passed, or maybe only one. There were moments, whole spaces of time, when he forgot what he was doing, where he was headed, even why he was in the water.

Teetering on the crest of a swell, he thought he saw the gleam of large metal drums. Part of a raft? Or just a bit of foam glistening in the relentless glare of sun? He tried to concentrate, to examine the dim shape before he sank into another trough. But all he could think of was how cold and tired he felt, how hard and uncomfortable his life jacket had become.

He struggled forward, forcing movement in arms and legs that had become bars of lead. Waves smacked into his face, stinging his eyes. And then, suddenly, the shadowy silhouette became clear. He was staring at one of the *Benlomond's* rafts: six watertight drums enclosed in a wooden frame about eight feet square.

It seemed close, but Lim had already learned how deceiving distances could be, and his crab-like way of swimming confused his sense of direction so that he was not always sure if he was making headway or swimming away from his goal.

The afternoon breeze quickened, whipping up waves that strangled him each time they broke.

Swallowed seawater cramped his stomach.

Overtaxed muscles in arms and legs twitched.

Rising and falling, rising and falling, he battled cold, drowsiness, a gentle voice that whispered the wind was blowing the raft closer and he could stop swimming and rest.

His head drooped, and he dozed, his mouth and nostrils barely above the water. Then a sudden choppy wave shoved the jacket sharp against his chin, jolting him awake, and he pushed on.

Until the gray mist descended again....

CHAPTER TWO

Huddled in his bunk, Lim could clearly hear the splash of water against the bow, feel the engines' pulsing, the distance between him and home stretching farther and farther.

The seventh of eight children, he was the last to leave. The red chair had carried his sisters to husbands in other villages before he was old enough to remember; the youngest had died as a baby, his second brother as a boy; and his other two brothers, Gee Hin and Gee Han, had been seventeen and thirteen when their parents sent them to Malaya — Gee Hin to clerk in an uncle's factory, Gee Han to work in a relative's grocery store.

The money they sent home allowed Lim to go to school. But the teacher was a mainlander who felt Hainan was a wilderness, and he spent most days reciting from the writings of officials exiled to Hainan long ago, punishing his students for his own inability to break out of the backwater. When Lim quit school shortly after he turned fifteen, he could read the newspaper, write a letter, keep simple accounts, recite the letters of the English alphabet and one or two common words and phrases, nothing more. But the six years he spent in school meant he had learned nothing about farming, and there was no other work in the village. So he idled his days fishing and kicking ball with other spoiled youngest sons.

He understood that eventually he would have to leave the village to find work. Nevertheless, he was totally unprepared when his father picked the last grains of rice from his evening bowl of gruel and announced, "Cousin Yee Tai is returning to Hong Kong tomorrow. You, Lim, will go with him."

Lim's mother was equally shocked. "But..."

"You know Gee Han's last letter said there would be an opening for a learn boy on his ship."

"But..."

"Lim is sixteen. With the Japanese advancing on the mainland, he can be conscripted any day. Luckily Yee Tai is willing to take him to Hong Kong to join the ship there."

Lim felt sick. It might be years before he could come home, perhaps never. Gee Han had been away seven years before he came back to marry and he had not been back since. Gee Hin, his oldest brother, had yet to come home at all. Lim's teacher said that was because life overseas was better, and he pointed out how quickly those who returned became restless, how anxious they were to leave the village with its crooked, unpaved streets, open gutters, and mud-brick houses. But Lim felt no such desire.

"I don't want to go," he blurted.

The lines creasing his father's forehead deepened. A martial arts master, he had spent his youth traveling from village to village, passing on his training wherever there were enough students to form a school. Even after his marriage, he had continued to travel and teach, becoming a farmer only when his own father died and there was no one else to plow the fields. For more than twenty years now he had been bound to the overworked soil, his wife forced to stretch the meager yield from one harvest to another by watering the rice into thin gruel, cooking and serving the tops of turnips and sweet potatoes — pig food — as vegetables. But he still found reasons to leave the village several times each year, and his impatience over his son's reluctance to leave was plain. Yet all he said was, "You're like a frog at the bottom of a well who thinks the patch of sky he sees is the whole world." Taking up his pipe, he stalked out the door.

Though his voice had been mild, his back, unbowed by years of labor, showed his implacable strength and will, and Lim knew that nothing would change his father's decision. But his mother hobbled after him on her bound feet, imploring.

As soon as they were out of hearing, Lim's sister-in-law bubbled, "Just think of it. You'll ride in wagons that don't need buffaloes or men to pull them. You'll eat meat with every meal. See moving pictures of real people flickering like shadow puppets on a screen. Lights that turn on by themselves and burn forever. All the things Gee Han has talked about...."

Gradually her enthusiasm spread to Lim, and it stayed with him through his mother's tearful goodbye and the half-day's walk to the jitney terminal. He had never ridden on anything faster than a water buffalo, and the novelty of the jitney ride to the port of Haikou and then the steamer to Hong Kong carried him through the next day and a half. But as his cousin dragged him up the gangway to the *S.S. Tanda,* Lim found himself wondering if the ship's officers would be kind or fierce, the work easy or hard.

His brother, in the stiffly starched uniform of a bar steward, left no room for doubts. "The European officers and crew give orders to the Chinese crew through a Chinese head man they call Number One, so it doesn't matter that you can't speak English. The engine crew are all Cantonese and you don't have to answer to them. But the Chinese in the catering department are from

Hainan Island and you are responsible to them all," Gee Han lectured sternly.

"You must be up at five to polish and sweep and set up the saloons, then bring up supplies from the hold. And all day, every day, you must be ready to work wherever you are needed, washing, scrubbing, fetching and carrying; stripping beds and making them up.

"The Chinese crew eats the passengers' leftovers, so we get breakfast and lunch after all the passengers are finished. Dinner is the crew's only meal that is not leftovers, and that is eaten at ten. But either the European cook that issues the stores or our own Chinese cook, or both, are skimming off the top, so you'd better not count on getting much. What you can count on is being in your bunk by eleven most nights and a salary of five Hong Kong dollars a month...."

Before Lim could absorb even half of it, the ship trembled under the first thresh of her propellers. Beneath his feet the deck rose in a long, swinging movement, then fell away as the ship's bow plunged, knocking him to his knees.

The ship — with cabins and dining and recreation rooms for 100 passengers, and cabins, mess rooms, and galleys for officers and crew as well — was overwhelming. Staggering through alleys and companionways as confusing as a maze, he found it impossible not to fall or get lost. Below decks was stifling. The smell of grease from the engines and the cooking in the galleys coupled with the constant motion of the ship was nauseating. When it came time to serve tiffin, one look at the hunks of meat and limp vegetables swimming in congealed gravy sent him hurtling in search of a place where he could vomit. It was the same at dinner.

Unable to face the crew's meal, Lim escaped to their quarters. Hidden under the covers of his bunk, the tears he had held back since leaving home streamed down his cheeks, and he buried his face in his pillow and sobbed.

He stopped as soon as he heard the men come in, but he was not quite quick enough.

"Look at the baby," they teased.

He tried to crawl deeper into the bedding, to wipe away his tears and mucus with the sheet. But a man grabbed his hands and held them up to the others, "Look at that. Soft as a whore's."

"A turtle without a shell."

Humiliated, Lim began to cry again. He searched the ring of faces for his brother's but could not find it. He was on his own.

Someone shoved a cigarette in Lim's mouth. "Here, suck this," he said, not unkindly. "It will make you feel better."

The smoke made him choke.

The men laughed, "What he needs is mother's milk."

Trying to swallow his sobs, Lim gulped more smoke, his own mucus, and he gagged. He had not eaten all day, so there was nothing to vomit, but once started, he could not stop the harsh, dry heaving....

Hoarse sobbing and whimpering shook Lim into confused wakefulness. Vomit crusted his mouth and nose, the decking on which he sprawled. Vaguely, he remembered fighting to reach the raft, waves buffeting him hard against it, his hands gripping the lifeline that becketed the sides, the terrible realization that there was no one on board, somehow climbing the three feet from water to deck alone. His teeth chattered and he shook uncontrollably with each new wash of water through the slats. Was there no way to get out of the sea's reach?

Ghostly clouds shrouded the moon so that he could not see. But every day for almost two years he had passed this raft when it was lashed to a mast on the *Benlomond*, and he snatched at bits of memory, what he could feel with his hands, piecing them together like parts of a puzzle until he saw the raft whole: two narrow ledges of open slat decking rising above the watertight drums which kept it afloat, a central well in between.

From the boards surrounding him and the water licking his flesh, Lim knew he was in the well, and he wanted to climb out, to take off the wet life jacket, the mess jacket and singlet clinging coldly underneath. But the ledges were not very wide and the raft rocked and he was afraid he might fall off.

Unexpectedly, he thought of the sampans and junks clustered around cargo ships in Hong Kong harbor, the men and women who worked the boats stepping nimbly across tiny decks crowded with hens stuffed in cages, children, babies tied to gourds.... If he could find a rope, the lanyard that had lashed the raft to the mast, and tie it around his waist, he would not sink or lose the raft if he fell.

He knelt cautiously. The raft had no reaction to the shift in weight. Then the rocking must be caused by the sea. He remembered how the swells had deepened as he swam, the force with which they had buffeted him against the raft. Was there a storm coming?

The possibility made his search for the lanyard more urgent. But his hands, shaking from cold and fear, found no sign of one. He tried again.

As the tips of his fingers worked around the raft a second time, he remembered looking for the lanyard earlier, while he was still in the water, using it to drag himself on board; and when he reached the third corner, his left hand bumped against a knot. He wrapped his fingers around it and pulled.

A rope slithered, dripping, across the ledge and into the well. Only five or six feet long, he could not loop it comfortably around his waist and still lie down. But he could tie it around an ankle. No, a wrist would be less awkward if he should fall. With fingers chilled numb, he worked the end of the rope into a clumsy noose then tugged at the straps and buckles binding his life jacket.

Wet and tightly knotted, they were impossible to untie in the dark. He bent his head to tear them loose with his teeth, but it was too awkward. Sucking in his breath, he tried to jerk the jacket over his head like a pullover. The long hours of soaking had made his flesh tender and his singlet squirmed up his chest and back as painfully as if he were peeling off a layer of skin. Anxious to get it over with, he clenched his teeth and pulled harder. Somewhere between his shoulders and the top of his head the jacket lodged, unmoving. Wet cloth encased his mouth and nose and he could not breathe. He yanked in one direction and then another. The jacket did not budge. Panicked, he tugged and ripped with teeth and nails.

Finally, he wrestled free. Panting as if he had been running for miles, he slipped the knotted lanyard around a wrist and climbed shakily out of the well and onto a ledge.

No water washed through the decking. But he was more exposed to the wind, the sharp bite of spray. The lump of wet, discarded clothing felt clammy as a corpse, and he kicked it aside, stuck his hands under his armpits and curled into a tight ball. Still the shivering did not stop.

The hard planks and the lanyard chafed. The motion of the raft and the lingering taste of vomit in his parched mouth made him queasy. Were those stars glimmering low on the horizon, or were they the glow of cigarettes from sailors on a submarine that had surfaced? Or were they the lights of a ship, of help on the way? He thought he heard the dull throb of engines, and he trembled, not knowing whether to call out or be silent, to hope for the bright glare of a searchlight sweeping the water or to fear it.

Peering anxiously into the dark, Lim felt as jumpy as a baby sleeping alone for the first time. He remembered his first night alone in a bed, a room of his own. Only six, he had thought every shadow a demon, and he had called for his mother in bed in the next room, the bed and room that had also been his until that night. He heard the soft thud of her quilt sliding to the floor as she rose, his father ordering her to stay.

Eventually, he had cried himself to sleep.

As he had done ten years later on the *S.S. Tanda.* His eyes brimmed with tears. His throat tightened. He was no longer a baby of six, or even a child of sixteen. He was twenty-four, a man.

Nevertheless, he wept.

CHAPTER THREE

Lim was aware of thirst, the need to relieve himself, an overwhelming sense of loss, the feeling of danger. And then he remembered. The *Benlomond* was gone. He was on a raft. Alone.

Unwinding stiffly from the tight ball in which he had passed the long, chill night, he eased himself down into the well, wincing as sore muscles protested and the lanyard tied to his wrist caught short and rubbed against broken skin. He untied the cord and rubbed grainy sleep from his eyes, hoping to find a ship, a lifeboat, another raft, any sign of human life besides his own.

Empty plains of sapphire blue water stretched out on every side. Though the morning sun was warm, Lim shuddered. Goosebumps mottled his skin, and he reached for his mess jacket. The narrow ledge he had slept on was bare. Quickly he scanned the well and the two ledges. His mess jacket and singlet and life jacket were gone.

Pressing his palms down on both ledges to steady him, he half stood, he was not sure why. Silver glinted between the slats of decking close to the far corner of the ledge. A button? He stepped forward to take a closer look. A buckle. A buckle from his life jacket which was hanging over the edge and would have already fallen were it not for the bit of metal caught in the crack.

Alarmed, Lim leaned over to grab it. The raft rocked, knocking him off balance. Instinctively he reached out for support, clutched air. Then he was sprawling across the ledge, too frightened to feel shame at the urine staining the deck beneath him.

The life jacket, a bright patch of orange, bobbed out of reach on swells so long and gentle the raft did not seem to be moving at all. But the sudden lurch had revealed the force beneath the languid surface, the ease with which the sea could claim him as well as the jacket, and he backed into the well as cautiously as if he were descending a cliff.

For a little while longer, the fleck of orange broke the endless sweep of blue. Then, sooner than he thought possible, it was gone, and there was nothing. Because there really was nothing? Or because his view was limited by the raft being so low on the water, almost a part of the sea?

Yesterday, swimming to the raft, he had thought that if he could only reach it, he would be safe. Now he was not sure. The central well where he crouched was about three feet by six. There was a compartment on either side, two metal containers fore and aft, and these encased him solidly, like the sides of a crib. But with water constantly sloshing through the open decking, lapping his feet and buttocks, he could not feel secure.

The ledges were worse. Running the full length of the raft, each ledge was probably about eight feet long. But they were only two, maybe two-and-a-half feet wide. Even with the lanyard tied around his wrist, he had lain rigid all night, terrified he might fall. And just now he had fallen. And lost his life jacket and clothes as well.

Trying to erase the chilly waves sweeping through him, he chafed his arms and legs, willing a ship or plane to appear. In a convoy, he would have been picked up by now. But since there had been no escorts, rescue would take longer. How much longer? No planes or ships would be spared to make a special search. But those in the area where the *Benlomond* had last sent out a position would surely have been alerted to look for survivors, and one of them would find him.

Thirsty, craving a smoke, he looked around him for supplies. The container directly in front of him had numbers and letters stenciled on it. He mouthed the sounds of the letters, stringing them together one by one. "10 G-A-L-L-O-N-S W-A-T-E-R" There was a large metal key secured to the tank with a lanyard. He edged forward, removed the key, and twisted the lid.

It resisted only slightly before giving way. Clear water sparkled, inviting, and he dropped the key to scoop some out, then realized the dirt and grease streaking his hands would taint the water. There had to be a dipper. He glanced at the metal container opposite, the two compartments under the ledges. None were labeled. He detached the key, crawled over to the other metal container, and wrenched it open. Inside was a treasure trove of tins, packages, and bottles, and on top of it all, a tiny, almost toylike measure at the end of a long handle.

Like a good omen, Lim's lucky guess cheered him, and he walked the few steps back to the water tank, his hands barely touching the sides of the well for support. Still standing, he dipped the measure, gulped thirstily. The sour aftertaste of vomit spoiled the first mouthful. He rolled the next around in his mouth, gargled, spat it out, once, twice, then realized the water was unpalatable because it was not fresh. But however unpleasant the taste, it eased his thirst, and he drank dipper after dipper.

Finally satisfied, Lim secured the dipper to the thwart above the water tank with the rope tie at the end of the handle. Then he squatted low again, not sure what he should do, wanting to search the metal container for cigarettes, to keep watch for a ship, to close his eyes and sleep until rescue came....

He wrapped his arms around his chest and hugged himself. If only he were on the raft with the other men, the tasks would be divided, one person to take charge of the supplies, one or two to keep watch while the others rested, told jokes, and cheered each other on.

Gripping a ledge, he hoisted himself up to look for the other raft. But the glare of sun on water was blinding, and he sank defeated. There had been five lookouts on the *Benlomond*, one aft, one on the flying bridge, two on the bridge, one at the bow, and they had apparently not sighted the submarine. A raft was so much smaller. Swimming towards it, he had lost sight of it often, though he had known it was there, the water was not rough, and the distance separating them not great. He would never find the other raft. Just as no one would see him. Not without signals.

Swivelling round on his heels, Lim squatted in front of the metal container where he had found the dipper and began sorting through the piles of tins and boxes. He unscrewed the lid of a large metal canister, found six cylinders wrapped in waterproofed paper. He unwrapped one. The short tube with a wooden handle the width of a broomstick looked rather like a fancy New Year's rocket. He examined it carefully, sighed. After six years of boat drills, he had not known how to lower a lifeboat. How would he set off a flare?

He noticed printing on the paper. Instructions? Kneeling, he smoothed out the paper on a ledge, laid the flare beside it, and sounded the words out one by one. When he reached the end, he started over again, and then again, pantomiming what he thought he should do.

It did not seem complicated. But the only way he could be certain he understood the instructions correctly would be to actually set off a flare, and there were so few. He picked up one of the two pots next to the canister. He had seen smoke pots thrown overboard during drills, and this one had a pin near the top that he guessed was a trigger. But again, without trying it, he could not be sure.

Fighting a rising panic, he set the pot down and picked up a long, heavy torch, relieved to have something familiar in his grasp. He pushed the switch. The glare made it impossible for him to tell if the torch was working. He cupped a hand around the circle of glass, shielding the bulb from the sun. It glowed reassuringly. At least he would have a light if he had to spend a second night on the raft. Now if he could only find some cigarettes. A smoke always calmed, always soothed, and as soon as he was less nervous, he would be able to think more clearly. Then the instructions for the signals would make more sense.

The next layer of packages and tins appeared to be food. There were words printed on some that were meaningless strings of letters. Others, like chocolate, evaporated milk, and sugar, he recognized immediately. Reading them, Lim realized he had not eaten since breakfast the morning before, and he was hungry. He opened the sack marked sugar, extracted a lump of barley sugar, and sucked noisily.

The delicious sweetness revived the feeling of luxury that the rare candy in childhood had brought, and he felt a childish excitement and curiosity as he divided the packages and tins into the known and unknown, then stacked them into neat piles on the two ledges above the central well. In the known piles, there were two pounds of chocolate, five tins of evaporated milk, one sack of barley sugar, and one bottle of lime juice. In the unknown, six boxes, ten tins, and one jar of tablets.

He picked up one of the flat, oval tins and sounded out the list of words printed on top: "PEMMICAN, DRIED BEEF, FLOUR, MOLASSES, AND SUET." Though he could not imagine them in combination, all except the first item were familiar foods in the *Benlomond's* stores, giving him the confidence to taste it.

Like the other tins, this one had a small key attached. He pried it off, worked loose the tail end at which an arrow pointed, threaded it into the "eye" of the key, then twisted it over and over until the narrow metal ribbon that sealed the tin was completely wrapped around it. He lifted the lid, dipped his index finger into the powdery substance, and licked suspiciously. It was salty, not at all unpleasant, in fact rather like beef essence. He dipped his finger in for a second taste. Three more dips and he replaced the lid and tried to open the jar of tablets.

The lid held fast. He knocked its lip against the decking, tablets rattling, until it loosened enough for him to unscrew. He recognized the word milk in the label "MALTED MILK," and the tablet he chewed reminded him of the Horlick's powder he used for fixing hot drinks for officers on evening watch.

Still crunching the last of the tablet, he opened one of the boxes, saw what looked like rectangular, dark brown biscuits. Something substantial at last! He bit into one eagerly. But as his teeth hit the solid, ungiving mass, he flinched, startled. Examining the biscuit, he saw his teeth marks barely dented the surface. The word "hard" in the label "HARDTACK" leaped out at him, and he nibbled more cautiously at a corner. Chips so tiny they were hardly worth the effort crumbled free. But if he soaked the biscuit in the sea like the officer with false teeth soaked his biscuits in tea, that should soften it enough for him to eat. The salt water might even give it flavor.

Leaning across the ledge to dip the piece he held, Lim's elbow knocked over the bottle of tablets, jostling the surrounding tins, the box of hardtack, the canister of flares. Biscuits tumbled across the deck and into the sea. For a moment, Lim stared, unable to move. Then, as though snapped out of a trance, he scooped up the packages and tins, stuffed them back into the metal container, twisted the lid tight, and collapsed into a corner of the well.

His head pounded and he cradled it with both his hands as though it might otherwise shatter. There was supposed to be a licensed deck officer on each life boat and raft, an officer to tell him what to do. Just as his parents, grandmother, school master, and other elders had directed him when he was a child. Just as his brother, the senior stewards, and officers had on the ships he served. All his life, there had always been someone to tell him what to do. But now, when he needed direction the most, when a single error in judgment could cost him his life, there was no one. In one night and a morning, he had lost his only clothing and his life jacket, and come close to losing all his provisions and his signals for help. If rescue did not come soon, how would he survive?

Shafts of afternoon sun bore down on Lim. His skin, glistening with sweat, prickled as if he were being eaten alive by ants. His eyes burned and his eyelids rasped painfully each time he blinked, distorting sea and sky into a single glittery blur.

He told himself the sun scorching him now was no fiercer than the one that had shone on him the day before, the one that had turned his village into a fiery furnace each summer. But yesterday clothing and steel bulkheads had shielded him. And at home there had been shade trees, the dim coolness of bricked rooms. All that shielded him now was the oil and dirt crusting his skin and the salt that stiffened his hair into a spiky, protective halo around his face.

Hoping there would be something he could use for a shelter in the compartments beneath the ledges, Lim knelt in front of one and unfastened the rope ties binding the latch. A pair of oars tumbled out on the deck. Oars?

There were no oar locks on the raft that he could remember. Sampans, which were propelled from the stern with a scull, had no oarlocks either. But they were long and light. The raft was square and heavy. He would never be able to move it alone.

He lifted the lid. Because of the airtight drums behind it, the compartment was shallow, its depth not much more than the width of the two oars. In it was a large roll of canvas, nothing else. He pulled it out. Yard after yard of narrow, blindingly white canvas filled the well.

Folding it into more or less equal lengths that stretched from the deck to his shoulders, Lim measured the fabric against himself. Since he was five feet eight inches tall, each length must be about five feet. He counted six folds. He was holding thirty feet of canvas.

Puzzled, he unlatched the opposite compartment. Neatly stacked one on top of the other were four poles and another roll of canvas. This piece was as wide as it was long, and there was a square hole in each corner with rope ties attached. One end of each pole was notched and had a hole just large enough to thread a rope tie through.

Reaching across one end of a ledge, Lim felt the corner, found a square hole just large enough to hold the base of a pole. The other three corners each had the same kind of hole. He had the makings of a shelter. His mouth twisted into a bitter grimace. The poles and awning were a cruel mockery, for alone, he would never be able to carry the poles onto the ledges and fit them into the holes without falling overboard.

He tried spreading the square piece of canvas across the well and lying underneath, with the roll of narrow canvas as a pillow. Release from the sun's relentless glare and the water licking his flesh gave the illusion of coolness. But in the dark there was nothing to do except fidget and worry. Wishing he had the makings for a smoke, he fingered the ugly weals around the wrist where he had tied the lanyard the night before, wondering what else he could secure himself with if he had to spend another night on the raft....

The closed space became stuffy. His feet and genitals began to swell from the long soaking. What if he refolded the roll of narrow canvas into a thick pad to raise him out of the water?

Lim pushed back the makeshift awning. Blinking against the sudden glare, he staggered to his feet, dropping the roll of canvas which unravelled in a tangled heap. Cursing, he rummaged through the pile of fabric, looking for an edge, a place to begin. He saw a corner and grabbed at it, found he held an edge with six grommets, each with a rope tie threaded through it. How had he missed them before? He searched excitedly for the other edge, laughed out loud when he saw that it too had six grommets with ties: If he wrapped the canvas around the raft, it would create a sort of wall that would keep him and his gear safe from any more spills.

Without help, wrapping the canvas around the raft was difficult but not impossible. Clutching the canvas with one hand and the wood slats of decking with the other, Lim squirmed across the narrow ledges on his belly and wound the canvas around the raft's edge inch by inch. Sweat blistered his back. His buttocks burned with an intensity he had not imagined possible. But eventually, the canvas circled the entire raft and he tied the two edges together.

The poles, six feet long, were too heavy and awkward to handle from the well. He heaved one onto the ledge and climbed up after it. Two-and-a-half feet of canvas rose like a solid wall above the raft's edge, but Lim remained cautious. And though it forced him to strain, he lifted the pole and maneuvered the heel into the corner while kneeling. There was no clamp, but the pole seemed sturdy enough, not wobbling in the slightest when he pushed hard against it.

One by one he set up the other three poles. His chest heaved and his breathing became short and ragged. Perspiration spilled out of every pore. He smeared the rivulets dripping down his face with his forearm and crawled into the well for a brief break.

Finally, he could not put off standing on the ledge any longer. Tying the lanyard around an ankle, he hugged a pole with one arm and dragged the heavy canvas up over his head with his other, struggling to fit the square hole at the corner over the top of the pole. The suffocating heat coupled with the strain and lack of food made Lim breathless and dizzy. But he had come too far to give up now, and he pushed on, fitting each corner of the canvas, then knotting them.

The result, a shelter that shaded yet allowed the passage of air and freedom of movement, filled him with pride. He thought of the topping-out ceremony that blessed a house when the main beam was raised or a new roof completed. He had no whole-cooked chicken, ceremonial buns, tea, or wine. No ritual candles, incense, or firecrackers. But he did have lime juice, sugar, and chocolate. And an exultation of achievement he had never known before.

Chocolate melted thickly on his tongue. Pemmican, savory and satisfying, followed. Then lime juice, pleasantly tart, making the lump of barley sugar all the more sweet.

An afternoon breeze caressed him. The harsh glare eased. Armed with his new-found confidence, Lim stood on the ledge and scrutinized sea and sky for the rescue he was sure would come soon.

CHAPTER FOUR

Night clouded Lim's optimism. Lying wide-eyed on a ledge, he thought he heard the sound of people talking, the throb of engines. But when he switched on the torch, he could find nothing, and the only sound was the slap of water against the raft.

His skin, hot from sunburn, made the damp night air seem twice as cold, and he could not stop shaking. Too late he understood why some seamen, fearful of a sinking, wore long, woolen underwear even in the tropics, and he bitterly regretted the carelessness that had lost him his singlet and mess jacket. Perhaps if he walked around a bit, he might feel warmer.

Arms wrapped around his chest, he started across the ledge. The moon hung like a white jade plate in a cloudless sky. The sea was flat. The canvas bulwark rose above the deck. Still Lim could not shake the fear that he might fall overboard, and his steps were as tentative as those of a woman with bound feet.

He thought of his mother hobbling in the kitchen and courtyard, his father, his sister-in-law. Was this same moon shining on them? Were they looking up at it and thinking of him? Were they alive? For three years after he left, he had sent letters home from every port and money as often as he could. But after the Japanese attacked Hainan in 1938, the letters from home stopped. It had been more than a year since he had heard from his brothers, Gee Han, who had left the sea to work as a translator in the Chinese army in India, and Gee Hin, who was under Japanese occupation in Penang. Was he, Lim, the only one left to continue the family line, to honor their parents' spirits with incense and food offerings?

The thought of spirits raised Lim's hackles, for the ghosts of those drowned became water specters, doomed to serve the Water Gods forever unless they trapped new victims into drowning in their place. So they hovered near rivers and oceans, seeking opportunities to blow hats and laundry into the water. Then, when the owner tried to recover his property, the specter would treacherously keep the object just outside his reach until the owner lost his balance and fell into the watery grave. Had water specters, the ghosts of his dead shipmates, rolled his life jacket onto the edge of the raft, then knocked him off his feet when he reached for it? Had they also dragged his singlet and mess jacket into the water and knocked over the box of hardtack? Were they poised nearby, waiting for a new opportunity to cause him to stumble and fall into the sea?

Longing for a cigarette, he considered opening the food tank and getting a lump of barley sugar to suck, dismissed it. What he wanted was the bitter taste and heady feeling a cigarette gave. Nothing else would satisfy. Crouching back down on the deck, he closed his eyes and conjured up his last smoke, the one just before the torpedoes struck, replaying each detail as though he were doing it now.

He took a cigarette paper and tobacco from the flat Navy Players tin in which they were stored, sprinkled the wad of tobacco diagonally across the thin square of white paper, and rolled it into a cylinder that was slightly wider at the end he would light. Then he ran his tongue across the loose edge of the paper and pressed it down lightly to seal. He struck a match. The pungent aroma of sulfur heralded the rush of pleasure that came with the first deep draw that lit the cigarette, pleasure that quickened as the smoke tantalized the delicate membranes of his tongue and inner cheeks, tunneled down his throat, and coursed through his lungs and nostrils in a perfect cycle of fulfillment.

Lost in his fantasy, Lim could almost imagine he was on the *Benlomond*, savoring those few minutes of private time late each night when his chores were done and he could escape on deck to smoke a cigarette alone. With every puff, the rough banter and easy laughter from the crew on the other side of the bulkhead receded, and he could forget the mingled odors of sweat and grease, the suffocation of shipboard living. Even as a child he had felt most comfortable in his own company, spending long afternoons hidden under the drooping fronds of weeping willows that edged the river bank, fishing. And he had disliked living in Hong Kong, the tiny dormitory the students shared, the crowded tenements and streets, where no escape was possible. But now he could think of nothing more pleasant than the sound of a human voice calling out a greeting, the feeling of flesh against flesh, warming.

Towards dawn, a thin layer of condensation covered the raft, adding to Lim's misery. Exhausted, his nerves strained taut by a night of broken sleep, he huddled in a corner, impatiently waiting for the sky to burst into color, the sun to shine down, warming, revealing a finger of smoke, the dark silhouette of a ship. Rescue.

Near the eastern horizon, the sky turned a pearly gray streaked with pink and blue. But to the northwest, clouds hung low and threatening. He climbed into the central well and leaned over the side to look directly above. Diffuse clouds hovered as though undecided whether to thicken or scatter. He thought he heard the low hum of a plane's engine, but a thorough search of the sky did not reveal the plane, and he wondered if what he had really heard was the distant rumble of thunder.

Was he imagining it, or were the clouds becoming darker? In the east, sky and sea joined in a dazzle of gold. No breeze stirred the warm, moisture-laden air or riffled the water. Yet he could not push back the doubts crowding in on him, and he found his lips moving in a silent, involuntary prayer to Tien Hau, Empress of Heaven and patron Goddess of boat people.

The raft rocked and Lim grabbed a ledge just in time to keep from falling. Thinking the storm had begun, he braced his legs for the next wave, but when he looked at the sea, it was as flat as it had been a few moments before. Were water specters playing tricks?

A second jolt knocked him against the corner of the well. As he fell, he thought he saw a large fish butting the raft, scratching its back against the side like a pig in a pen. Steadying himself, he scanned the water around him, saw a dark triangular fin starboard. A shark?

His only experience with sharks had been on a beach in Hong Kong. He was sitting on the sand, minding his fellow students' clothes while they swam, when the lifeguard suddenly rang a bell and everyone headed for shore. People began shouting, "Sharks! Sharks!" and when Lim looked where they pointed, he saw one dark triangular fin, then two more. No one was hurt that day, but on their way back to the school, the boys had talked of slow swimmers who had lost a leg or an arm, even their lives. The images their stories had inspired haunted Lim, and he scrambled up onto a ledge.

Where had the shark come from? How long had it been there? Was it this shark and not a sudden swell or a water specter that had bumped the raft yesterday? Or was it another shark? And if it was a shark and he had not seen it, then were there also ships and planes that had come and gone without his notice?

He scoured the sea for another fin, saw none. But sharp little puffs of hot air were scurrying across the smooth surface aft, churning isolated bursts of foam that rippled into dark cat's-paws, signaling a hardening wind, a squall.

The well was the logical place to ride out a squall, and he did not think a shark's snapping jaws could reach him through the decking. Yet he could not make himself climb off the ledge. Only a few weeks before in Capetown, he had heard of a Chinese steward rescued from a similar raft after three days. His thighs bore the marks of shark's teeth. And he was completely mad.

Then he remembered the lanyard. Tying it around his wrist, he lay flat on the ledge on his belly, ready to cling to the decking the minute the squall broke. He tried to pray again to Tien Hau, but words would not come. Closing his eyes, he willed her presence, saw her as he had the very first time, when he was seven.

Since their village lay inland, his father went twice, sometimes three times a year to the ocean to buy fish to bring back to market, and after years of begging, Lim finally persuaded his father to take him. While his father bargained with the fishermen, Lim watched, mesmerized, as endless skeins of silken foam danced ashore, teasing the clefts between his toes before bubbling merrily into the hot sand beneath his feet.

As far as he could see, the tips of waves sparkled like priceless jewels, and he waded into the water to scoop them up. But no matter how tight he made his fists, the golden drops slid between his fingers. Frustrated, he burst into tears.

To distract Lim, his father took him to the temple dedicated to Tien Hau. But the black eyes and face of the Goddess and her grotesque attendants, Thousand League Eyes and Favoring Wind Ears, frightened Lim, and he began to cry again. His father explained that Tien Hau's black face meant she was impartial, unselfish, and dispassionate in her relations with other women, capable of treating all men with equal concern. But Lim was too young to understand, and only when his father began telling him the story of Tien Hau's first miracle did he finally stop crying.

She was seven, he said, the very same age as Lim, when her father and two brothers were overtaken by a storm at sea. Though she was home talking to her mother, she sensed their danger, the ship pitching and tossing in all directions, the passengers pale with terror. So her soul left her body, and in an instant, she swooped her brothers into her arms, her father into her mouth, and flew to shore.

Her mother — terrified when her daughter broke off in the middle of a word, her body becoming stiff and cold — began to weep, crying for her daughter to wake up. Touched to the heart, the girl answered. But when she opened her mouth to speak, she dropped her father and he drowned. Instead of reproaching her mother, the girl took pity on the widow and refused to marry so she could care for her until her death.

Lim felt water rushing through the decking in the well, the raft tossing up and down. Tightening his grip around the planks, he raised his head just high enough to peer over the bulwark. The sun had vanished. Dark green swells, slate gray in the troughs, rolled in from a horizon that rose and fell. Lightning ripped through the purple black clouds staining the sky, letting loose torrents of rain. There was a deep drum roll of thunder, and suddenly the squall was racing towards him with all the menace and fury of a cavalry of frothing stallions charging a defenseless foe.

He twisted his head away, caught a glimpse of the eastern sky shining golden, like a promise from Tien Hau. Surely a Goddess who had shown such compassion and power as a child would be even more merciful now that she was Empress of Heaven?

Shrill gusts of wind skinned the tops off mounting swells and lashed the canvas bulwark and awning, tugging at the rope ties. Lim tried to whistle, but no sound came. Bile rose harsh and bitter in his throat. Clenching his jaws, he forced himself to swallow.

Rain pelted down. Waves slammed the sides of the raft. Spray and wind-whipped rain stung. The lanyard chafed his wrist. Splinters dug into his palms. His muscles cramped from the tension. But he dared not move.

Then, just as suddenly as it had begun, it was over. The wind that had brought the squall swept it towards the far horizon; the raft was riding a rapidly flattening sea; and a rainbow arced in a brilliantly colored bridge that linked sea and sky. Yet he felt no relief. For he now fully understood his helplessness should a true storm come before rescue.

CHAPTER FIVE

For hours after the squall, Lim thought every play of light on water the shadow of a shark's fin. Then he mistook a whale for a submarine, recognizing it only when it shot geysers of water into the air. The whale dove, and Lim worried that it might come up under the raft and flip it over. He knew the open-slat decking that surrounded the metal drums was exactly the same on top and bottom so the raft would always land correctly no matter how it was thrown from a ship. But now that he had put up the poles and awning, what could he do to prevent their loss? And would he be more secure tethered to the raft by the lanyard or floating free?

Relief flashed as the whale shot out of the water about fifty yards distant, its back shimmering gold in the late afternoon sun. But when it moved ponderously around the raft, circling, Lim began to fret, relaxing only when, with a thunderous snort, it made off, leaving a long, slimy brown trail of excrement.

Again his relief was short-lived. Three fish shaped like torpedoes lunged near the raft, banging it, knocking him off balance. Only three or four feet long, these fish could not upset the raft, and the canvas bulwark kept him from falling overboard. But their presence made him nervous, and unlike the whale, these fish remained, though they were not always visible.

In the dark, the moisture the sun had drawn up during the day returned in heavy condensation. The night wind cut quick and deep. Shivering, dreaming of a hot bath, Lim was sure he saw telltale slivers of light from blacked-out portholes, the dark bulk of an oncoming steamer. He heard the sound of an engine, men's voices. Quickly he turned on the torch to signal his presence. Something flew out of the water, twitched, flicked against his hand. He screamed, dropped the torch, saw in the rolling slash of light across the deck a flying fish gasping for air. Feeling foolish, he tossed the fish back into the sea and prayed for dawn.

In the morning, he tied three knots in the lanyard, two for the days he had already endured, one for the day just begun. He had no appetite. Yet he knew he must eat. To make the hardtack palatable, he tried crushing one in a tin with the heavy water tank key, then mixing the crumbs into a thick soup with water and a bit of pemmican for flavoring. The rhythmic grinding soothed just as the steady, circular motion of ink stick against stone had comforted during his school days, and he added another biscuit and then another to the tin to prolong the moment of solace.

Eating the soupy mess offered no such pleasure. No matter how hard he swallowed, each lumpy spoonful stuck in his throat like tong yuen, the tasteless dumplings his grandmother used to make. When he added more water to the mixture, the paste stuck to the roof of his mouth like glue, and neither water nor tongue could dislodge it. He scraped the sticky mess free with his fingers and gargled.

Giving up his attempt to eat, he went over the instructions for the flares once again. Then, making sure the signals were within easy reach at the top of the container, he scoured sea and sky. A shoal of flying fish glided effortlessly above the water, their fins shimmering silver. Suddenly they leaped. Fins beating, they soared, then landed, then soared again, like the flat stones he used to skip across the stream at home. As they passed starboard, he realized they were being chased, leaping to get out of reach of snapping jaws. Sharks?

Clinging to a corner pole, Lim scrambled to his feet for a better look. Sleek and golden blue, the fish chasing the flying fish cut through the water with the speed and sharp precision of speed boats, leaving long white wakes. They stopped exactly where the flying fish touched down, and for a few seconds the water churned madly. Then the flying fish took off once more, beating their fins and using their tails to pick up speed. But again the large golden blue fish outdistanced their prey and were waiting when the flying fish touched down, and the water roared as they fought like dogs over scraps.

Though the golden blue fishes' jaws opened wide as any shark's and the water boiled as they fought over their victims, they somehow did not seem as menacing, perhaps because they ignored him. And as one day ground into another with no sign of rescue, he began to look forward to their arrival.

Finally, on the sixth morning, shortly after he had tied another knot in the lanyard, he sighted a ship. At first it was only a blur on the horizon. Then the silhouette sharpened, sinking and rising with the swells, her thin spiral of smoke the only constant.

His belly leaping with excitement, Lim jumped into the well, grabbed a flare from the container, and climbed back up onto the deck. The ship was gone.

Reason told him that a real ship would not have vanished, that the smoke and silhouette had been a mirage. But his eyes raked the sea. It wasn't possible that so many days had gone by without a single ship or plane. Unless the *Benlomond* had sunk too quickly, or the radio operator had been hurt, or the transmitter damaged so that no distress signal had gone out.

Lim sagged into the well, defeated. If there had been no distress signal, no one would be aware that the *Benlomond* had sunk until the ship became overdue. Wartime schedules were hard to keep, so the port authorities would probably not be concerned until she was several days late. That meant that it might be ten or more days from the time she sank before a call went out to ships and planes to search for survivors. Meanwhile he was drifting farther and farther from where they would look.

Automatically he reached up to his chest to get the makings of a cigarette from a pocket, found only naked flesh. Frustrated, he fidgeted with the wiry bristles darkening his jaw, fighting the urge to go through the compartments in the raft's well.

Twice now he had dreamed there were tins of tobacco and cigarette papers hidden behind the oars. The first time, when he had wakened, he had actually searched the compartments. Of course they were not there. In the second dream, he saw them again, but before he could pick them up, they were caught and scattered in a sudden gust of wind, and he had not been able to save one paper, one bit of tobacco.

Desperate, he broke off a lump of barley sugar and bit down hard. But the sweet only deepened his craving for a cigarette, and the hunger consumed him, cramping his belly, his ability to concentrate, to think.

The sea, the heat closed in on him, and he felt as though he were in the fireroom where the crew hung their wash to dry. When he stepped over the casing, a rush of suffocating heat slammed into his face and chest, punching the air out of his lungs. Watching the firemen, their gleaming sweat-slick skin fiery red and hot as the coals they shoveled, he had often wondered how they stood the white heat blasting out at them from the open furnace doors. Now he realized they stood it, as he did, because they had no choice. And because relief would come. For them, at the end of their watch. For him...

CHAPTER SIX

By the seventh day Lim had learned to brace his legs against the heave of the raft as it met a swell, and he did not stumble even when the raft rode in deep water, or a fish banged against the side. But the monotony and brevity of the walk caged him in. Three paces covered the full length of the deck, forcing a turn. Another three paces, another turn. Kneeling, he leaned over the canvas bulwark and splashed water over his head and shoulders.

The sea rippled like a dragon flexing its muscles, and the short, unpredictable waves made him edgy. Wherever the breeze shattered the top of a choppy little whitecap, tiny, iridescent rainbows shimmered in puffs of spray. Flying fish skimmed across the surface adding their own sheen to the glitter.

There was a barely discernable flurry. The fish scattered, hopping across the sea like grasshoppers chased by a farmer. Lim looked for the golden blue fish, found a single line of shadow darkening the water. The edge of a triangular fin? No, a narrow tube. The top of a periscope.

He dropped down behind the bulwark, peered over the edge. The periscope and the top of a conning tower were clearly visible above a blur of unusual swells. He ducked low again.

Chewing his lips, the insides of his cheeks, he wondered what he should do. Just as all surface vessels on the Atlantic were Allied, the submarines were bound to be German. At best he would become a prisoner of war....

The oppressive knot in Lim's chest swelled. The sailors on the submarine that had sunk the *Benlomond* had aimed their guns at him, but they had not actually fired. And he had heard of enemy commanders who sometimes gave cigarettes to castaways....

Blood from his nervous chewing filled Lim's mouth. Swallowing hard, he crouched nervously, ready to sprawl flat again in an instant.

The morning breeze seemed to have withered, taking with it the choppy waves, and he could see brightly colored fish swimming in a strangely clear streak twenty feet away. In the distance, the water gleamed with a fiery polish. Closer, there were dull bronze patches scarred with foam that glinted crystal when his eyes teared from the glare. But there was no submarine.

His head spun in a kaleidescope of relief, regret, hope. He remembered how quickly his bright orange jacket had vanished. And a periscope tube was so slender. But he had seen it. And the top of a conning tower too. And a submarine on the prowl meant shipping was likely to be close.

Desire turned bits of cloud into corkscrews of smoke, a torpedo fish into a submarine, and he began to wonder if the periscope had also been a mirage, a trick of hungry ghosts.

There had been so many ships torpedoed, so many men killed violently, their ghosts forced to wander like tramps in search of charity. And vagrant ghosts were often mean, possessing terrible powers of revenge. Could they be punishing him for living when they had died, torturing him with mirages, keeping him away from the shipping lanes?

The afternoon wore on.

The heat and glare intensified.

His eyes burned.

His head buzzed.

He slumped into the well. Water slopped through the slats, cooling. But afraid he might miss a ship, he dared not stay.

To the south, a dark speck blotted the gold. Instantly Lim's pulse quickened, and he wanted to dive into the well to light a flare. At the same time he was afraid the stain was another mirage that would vanish if he so much as blinked. Scarcely breathing, he tracked the smudge, his excitement and confidence growing as it took on the squat shape of a tanker, then sharpened into the clean strong lines of a destroyer.

Suddenly it blurred. Lim blinked, rubbed his eyes. The silhouette shattered entirely. Panicked, he rubbed harder, shook his head. Slowly the confusing dazzle of black and gold and red dots dissolved, and he saw the ship again, a tramp high in the water. She was still too far away for the watch to see his signals. But he was too impatient, too afraid of losing her to wait until she came closer, and he leaped into the well to get them.

He decided to set off a smoke pot because it seemed easier and more likely to attract attention to his general area. When the ship came closer, he would use the flares to indicate his specific location. He grabbed a smoke pot, dropped it. Cursing, he scooped it up with both hands and rubbed it dry against his chest.

Breathing a prayer to Kwan Yin, the Goddess of Mercy, he pulled what he hoped was the firing pin and hurled the pot into the sea. A dense red orange smoke, more beautiful than the loveliest dawn, billowed from the pot, and Lim laughed, exultant. The men on watch could not fail to notice this strange, bright cloud spreading slowly towards them.

He could not see the ship through the thick orange haze and he shifted from one foot to the other, praying the smoke would remain and mark the raft as long as possible, praying it would quickly dissipate so he could see the ship again.

Within a few minutes, the cloud thinned, revealing the ship, her course unchanged.

Lim snatched the canister of flares and twisted open the lid. The flare he had already unwrapped slid out. He grabbed it by its handle, aimed it so it would shoot towards the ship, and ripped off what he thought was the firing tape. The cap came off with the tape. Nothing else happened.

He glared at the cap in one hand, the flare in the other. There was a scratch surface like the flinty sides of a match box on the top of the cap, and a dark head, the size of a thumb tack, on the tip of the flare. As though the flare were a huge match, he struck it against the flinty scratch surface.

Nothing happened.

He tried again.

It sparked, and he tossed it high. It soared in a wide arc, then sank unlit.

For a moment, Lim stared, immobilized by the dimple in the water where the flare had sunk, fulfilling his darkest fears. Then he tried to reread the instructions, to figure out what he might have done wrong. The printed letters ran together in a senseless muddle. He tried sounding out the letters. But he was too unnerved by his failure to concentrate.

Had the salt air and moisture corroded the flare? Or had he thrown it too soon? Perhaps he should not have thrown it at all. Or maybe he was lighting it incorrectly. No, that at least was certain or it would not have sparked. And without matches, there was no other way to ignite it.

Finally he decided to strike the next flare the same way, but this time he would not throw it into the sea. He shook the canister. Several flares slid out. He was too rushed, too upset to get a proper hold, and they slipped from his grasp. He doubled over to catch them. But he was not quite quick enough, and one of the flares shot between the slats of the well, sinking into the depths below.

Tears pricked Lim's lashes. Blood raced, gorged his head. Still doubled over, he tottered backwards onto the ledge behind him so that he could hold the canister over the safety of his lap. Fingers trembling, he shoved the flares back in. Except one.

He returned the canister to the food tank for safe-keeping. Then, gripping the flare by the wood handle, he ripped off the waterproof wrapper and tugged at the tape until it jerked free. Muttering another prayer to Kwan Yin, he inverted the cap and scraped it across the upper end of the tube. Once. Twice.

A short white flame flared, and a red ball rose with a hiss, the glare blinding. Sparks fell on Lim's hand, the deck. Instinctively he sucked his fist, stamped the boards beneath his feet. But he scarcely noticed the sharp licks of pain, for the ball was soaring high above the water then bursting in a shower of bright red stars.

All too soon the brilliant sparkles faded, and his joy and thanks to Kwan Yin died with the flare. The ship was still plowing ahead on the same course. He glanced at the sky, the sun dipping towards the horizon. It must be just after tea time, when most of the crew would be smoking, chatting, writing letters, mending clothes, or just sitting. But where were the watch, the officers on the bridge?

She was close enough now for him to hear the beat of her engines, and the throbbing became an extension of his own heartbeat as he jiggled out another flare, tore off the paper, and yanked the tape. Leaning over the side so the sparks would fall harmlessly into the sea, he tilted the tube, struck it against the cap. The flare shot up and hung, a splash of red in the blue flame of sky. The burning particles drifted down, sizzling as they sank into the sea.

He held his breath as the ship continued on course.

Then, heaving to, she steered straight towards him, throwing aside sheets of spray as she ploughed through the sea.

He had been seen! Before nightfall he would be safe and clean, eating real food, smoking real cigarettes, and drinking tea. Leaping and shouting his joy, he waved at the ship. Everything about her was beautiful, the low flush hull, the drab gray superstructure, the swaying life boats, the smoke billowing from the single funnel, even the guns fore and aft.

Breathless, he paused, felt a stirring in the air, a quickening in the water. He looked at the ship, the sun sinking in the west. Would she reach him before dark? Even dusk might be treacherous. And if the breeze that was stirring hardened into a wind, it could whip the water into swells that would make him less visible, the transfer from the raft more difficult.

He shuddered, remembering a friend who had lost his life while being transferred onto a rescue ship from a lifeboat that had swamped and capsized. The raft would do neither, but seven days of eating little more than sugar and chocolate and pemmican had sapped his strength, and he was not sure that in a rough sea he could climb a rope ladder or net without falling.

Gradually the ship steamed nearer.

He knew the closer she came, the slower, the more careful she would have to be to prevent running him down. But it seemed to Lim she was not moving at all, though the curl of foam thrown back by the bow was plain, and he set off a fifth flare to spur her on.

It shot into the air where it formed a bright, luminous trail. There was a short, flattish beat, the slow lazy sound of engines idling. Three men appeared on the bridge, a handful at the rails, the gun platform. How exciting it was to see so many people, to hear voices.

He caught the glint of binoculars flashing from the bridge, searching the sea. Was it possible that he still had not been seen?

He set off his last flare, then leaped and waved and shouted beneath its fiery glow.

Suddenly he realized he was being studied.

He knew that enemy submarines sometimes attacked rescue ships, and recently some had even launched rafts with men pretending to be shipwrecked. Then, when a ship approached to rescue the men, she was torpedoed. Did the men examining him think he was a decoy?

He pointed to his sunken cheeks, the patches of sunburn on brown skin streaked with grease and grime, the scruffy beginnings of a beard, his dry, cracked lips — proof that he was a true castaway and not a decoy. "I from *Benlomond*," he shouted. "Sink seven days. Help!"

Dropping to his knees, he held his hands up in supplication, repeating the same cry over and over until it became a chant. To the men passing the binoculars back and forth. To Kwan Yin, any Goddess or God or man who would heed his cry.

The engines revved back into life, and Lim leaped to his feet, froze as the ship swung around and changed course. Swells rocked the raft, knocking him off balance. He sprawled on the ledge. Dazed, he clutched a corner pole. The ship was so close, he could hear the thud of a hatch closing, a stifled curse, the swish of hose pipes as the crew washed down the decks, a man's cough. Surely he could swim to it.

He swung one leg over the bulwark. What if he lost the ship and the raft as well? His skin turned clammy in a sudden burst of cold perspiration, and he teetered on the edge, one leg on either side of the bulwark, unable to leap into the sea, unable to give up the chance for rescue.

Then he remembered he had one more smoke pot. He jumped into the well, snatched it out of the food tank, jerked the firing tape, and flung it at the wake of the disappearing ship.

Smoke spread like spilled blood.

The red cloud wreathed, spluttered into ignominous death.

The ponderous swells the ship had created when she swung around disappeared.

The sound of engines died.

Her smoke became indistinguishable from the clouds.

And then she was gone, and it was as though she had never been.

CHAPTER SEVEN

All the humiliations, the bitterness Lim had swallowed since leaving home welled up in him, and he shook his fists at the empty horizon, cursing the men who had denied him.

"May crows pick out your eyes!"

"May fish devour you!"

"May fish be your coffin and water your grave!"

"May you die by drowning and your body never be found by friends!"

His puny cries only emphasized his impotence and he sank onto the ledge, spent and defeated.

In his darkest moments, he had acknowledged the possibility that neither ship nor plane would cross his path. Or they might pass without seeing his signals. Or he might become a prisoner of war. It had never occurred to him that he would be seen, that a ship would come so close and then refuse to take him on board.

There was no mistaking the rejection. All too clearly he had seen the ship change course after his signals were sighted, felt the binoculars' glassy stare, the deliberate turning away. Yet he had almost jumped overboard to swim after her. And he had thrown his last signal in her wake. For to admit the truth was to destroy hope. And without hope there was only death.

Six years out of the village, Lim thought himself stripped of all illusions. But he saw now that he had fooled himself about the Allies the same way a villager was fooled by the talk and gifts of emigrants returning from abroad.

They always brought wonderful things. Special metal bottles that kept boiled water hot for hours. Pens that held ink and did not need to be dipped. And their talk was full of good times. The ease with which one could make a living. The unique abilities and strange, almost childlike qualities of foreigners. The houses stacked one on top of another. Black boxes with handles you could speak into and be heard by people in distant cities. Listening to them, the villagers were filled with awe and envy. Some young farmers decided to leave so they could experience the wonders for themselves. Others, like Lim and his brothers, were forced to go by parents who wanted their sons to have the comforts they had never known.

As a learn boy, Lim had been on call at all hours, fetching and carrying until he was so exhausted he staggered on his rounds more asleep than awake. But the emigrants' talk that he had heard all his life had been so convincing that for months he believed no one else on board was working as hard or as long and for so little money. Neither did he make the connection that his fellow stewards were the emigrants he and other villagers had looked up to in awe. At first because he had been too homesick to notice anything except his own misery. And then because the difference between the blank faces, empty grins, stooped heads, muted voices, and pidgin English of the Chinese crew and the proud swagger and bold, confident talk of the returning emigrants was too great. Eventually, however, he became aware of the angry grumbles of the men around him, their unhappiness over the long hours, leftover food, poor pay, and the refusal to allow Chinese any positions except the most menial; and he recognized that their frustrations reflected his own.

Thinking back, he suddenly realized how old most of the emigrants were before they came home to retire, how few were able to build big houses or buy more land. And there were those who returned broken, a burden on their families, or died miserable deaths away from home, their widows forced to take up the work of men in order to support their families.

When Lim asked his brother why he did not protest the unfairness of working unlimited hours for one-third the wages of his British counterpart, his brother said, "Conditions aren't so bad on this ship. On some, the officers beat the Chinese crew."

In the crowded cabin the catering crew shared, there were no private conversations. The man who slept above Lim swung down and sat on the edge of the bunk.

"It wasn't always like this," he explained. "Long before you were born, the Chinese seamen in Liverpool organized a collective to fight against racial discrimination by British sailors. We also fought for higher wages and better working conditions."

"Don't forget those blood-sucking Chinese labor contractors who work for the shipping companies," another man added.

"Those were the days," the old timer in the next bunk sighed. "Imagine, 50,000 Chinese seamen on strike!" He paused. "Let's see... that was in '22, in Hong Kong."

The man sitting beside Lim shook his fist. "We held out for two months, and we won!"

"Then why are conditions so bad now?" Lim asked.

The men turned on him.

"Listen to the tadpole."

"Still crying for his mother's tit and he thinks he can criticize."

Confused by the men's abrupt change, Lim stammered, "But I..."

His brother closed his hand over Lim's mouth, his touch firm, but not unkind. "There's been a world depression for the last few years. Thousands of seamen, British and Chinese, have been laid off. Companies have cut their crews to the bone, replacing men who have worked for years with apprentices, learn boys like you."

Silenced, Lim had said no more. But he had watched and listened. A year went by. Two. Then three, and he saw that though general conditions improved, the lot of the Chinese seamen did not. But he also heard that in America, the Gold Mountain, things were different. There was a National Maritime Union there that included Chinese workers. They went on strikes together, and together they won. The union even came out in support of China's war of resistance, joining Chinese seamen in refusing to ship scrap iron to Japan.

None of that helped Lim or the other Chinese on British ships, however, and he quit the sea. Months later, when his cousin advised Lim to sign articles for the *Benlomond,* he said that the need for Chinese seamen had forced British companies to limit the hours worked by the catering department and to increase their pay.

On ships like the *Benlomond,* the new improvements were observed. Lim's pay, though two-thirds the rate of a British seaman, was $80 a month, sixteen times more than his wages as a learn boy. The crew slept two to a cabin. The food was not bad. And with no passengers, the work was light, leaving plenty of free time to smoke, play cards, riffle through a newspaper, sleep.

Satisfied, his one act of rebellion over, Lim closed his ears to the complaints of Chinese seamen on other ships whose demands for equal treatment were often met with refusals, sometimes even violence. And so he had ended up fooling himself, believing that all he needed to do was to catch the attention of an Allied ship and he would be picked up, rescued, saved. How could he have been so gullible?

The men examining him could not possibly have believed he was a decoy or the ship would not have come so close. Rather, they had deliberately decided not to pick him up after they saw he was Chinese.

"Why risk our own lives by staying in sub-infested waters to rescue him?" they had probably said. "It's just a Chinaman."

For the first time since the *Benlomond* had sunk, Lim was glad he was alone and not on the raft with the other men. With most of the Chinese working below decks where the torpedoes had hit, the men on the raft were most likely English. The gunners perhaps, or the lookouts. They had treated him fairly enough on board the ship, but men trapped together in a desperate situation sometimes changed. What if they expected him to serve them still, or gave him less food? There might be misunderstandings because of language. Or personality clashes. Fights perhaps. Even death. Alone he had only himself to consider. And he would survive.

There would be other ships. And one of them would have a Master with the courage, the compassion to stop and pick him up no matter how high the risk. Or the watch on an American ship would see him. With a seaman's union that included Chinese as its members, surely they would not pass him by. Or a pilot on a plane would find him. Or he would drift to land. And when the war was over, the Japanese army of occupation gone, he would go back to his village loaded with gifts, a story that would amaze.

Lim closed his eyes.

Mists slithered down velvet green mountains, settling low, moist, and cool over burgeoning fields that promised rich harvests. Trees hung heavy with fruit. The fragrance of black, loamy soil, blossoms, and ripe fruit mingled with the earthier smells of compost and night soil.

Seated on a bamboo stool just outside his father's house, Lim rolled and lit a cigarette. Puffing slowly, he contemplated the festival meal that weighed pleasantly in his belly. Clear soup shiny with pearls of fat. Hainan chicken, fresh, tender, and crispy as only his mother could make it. Bitter melon, pale green and warty, sliced and stir fried with a bit of dried shrimp. Grayish purple slices of taro bedded between fat pork slices and steamed. And bowl after heaping bowl of fluffy white rice.

The sow snuffled and lumbered behind the front wall, her piglets squealing after her, and the chickens scattered, squawking, making way for Lim's father and mother and sister-in-law, the villagers that were gathering as they always did whenever an emigrant returned. They loaded the table beside Lim with platters of sliced pineapple, coconut, mango, and sugar cane; bowls heaped with lychees; pitchers of coconut milk; and steaming pots of tea, then settled themselves on the stools they had brought.

Lim cracked the brittle red shells of lychees and sucked the tender white flesh within. He sampled the sliced fruit, his tongue darting quick as a lizard's to catch the sticky sweet juices dribbling down fingers and chin. Finally, when he could eat no more, he leaned back against the wall, rolled and lit another cigarette, and inhaled deeply. Then he began to speak. Though he had always been a less talk person, words rolled off his tongue, and the villagers leaned forward, open mouthed, gasping, laughing, sighing....

As he spun the gossamer threads that made up his fantasy, Lim remembered and added new details of the home and village he had not seen since he was a boy. The smell of smoky kitchen fires. The bright chirrup of cicadas hidden in tall grasses. The fleeting shadows of birds winging home to nests in trees and beneath eaves.

The special way their neighbor's daughter had of shaking her thick braid like a filly proudly tossing her mane.

Each memory added to the reality of his dream. The sharp edges of pain and loss became submerged in a blossoming assurance that he would be saved, and he slept more deeply and restfully than he had since the *Benlomond's* sinking.

CHAPTER EIGHT

Lim woke refreshed. He recognized now that since the torpedo had struck, he had acted almost entirely on impulse. If he were to survive, he could no longer live from moment to moment. He had to plan, to make up for earlier carelessness, to avoid new mistakes.

Maintaining a daily watch was obviously essential. But what would he signal with? The torch could be used at night, but he was much more likely to need a signal during daylight. Could the circle of glass shielding the bulb in the torch be used as a signal mirror? Aiming the glass towards the sun, he tried to make it flash. It winked so weakly in the sun's brilliant glare that even the sharpest eyes would have trouble distinguishing it from the general glitter. But it would have to do.

Lim turned his attention to his food and water supplies. At home in the village, water had to be carried from the well to the house two buckets at a time, and on board ship, water had to last from port to port. Minimal consumption was a habit, and he had generally restricted his drinking to sunrise and sunset and once or twice during the heat of the day.

The level of the tank seemed to be down about one fifth. That meant he had drunk approximately two gallons in seven days. If he continued to drink as much, the water would last twenty-eight more days. But if he reduced his consumption to one pint a day, it would last twelve additional days.

Remorse over his earlier optimism made Lim cautious, and he decided to try and stretch both the water and food supply for forty days. Carefully, he inventoried each item. Almost a full box of the hardtack was gone though he had actually eaten fewer than a half-dozen biscuits. There was less than half a sack of sugar, a pound of chocolate, a little over eight tins of pemmican, almost a full jar of malted milk tablets, one-third of the bottle of lime juice, and all five tins of the milk. Dividing by forty, he came up with a daily ration of one measure of evaporated milk, six biscuits, half a measure of pemmican, and two malted milk tablets. He did not figure the chocolate, sugar or lime juice into his calculations. Until they ran out or he was picked up, he would save them for treats for when he felt low.

Since he had no appetite, Lim did not think he would be hungry. But he would almost certainly lose additional weight, and the hard wood ledge that was uncomfortable as a bed now would become unbearable. In addition to padding, he needed a cover to protect him from the cold and spray, the shivering that rubbed raw tender patches of sunburned skin and knotted the muscles in his legs into painful cramps.

The mess jacket and singlet would have helped some. The life jacket, picked apart, would have been ideal. But the only fabric he had was the burlap wrapped around the lime bottle, the canvas awning and bulwark. The scrap of burlap was too small and coarse, the awning too critical to consider. But the bulwark?

The raft rode the swells smoothly. During the nights, he had not once rolled against the bulwark or into the well. So long as the weather held, the likelihood of falling overboard seemed slim. But what if a squall or storm took him by surprise? Would he be safe without a bulwark then?

Never having been in this part of the world before, he had no idea what kind of weather to expect. So far, the only consistency had been the fierceness of the sun during the day and the chill at night, so that he was either unpleasantly hot or uncomfortably cold. There might be one day of light breeze, then two or three of dead calm. But whenever a squall blew up, the sharp wind that brought it also whipped up quick, nasty little waves. They seemed to be only surface waves that rode over the ground swells, often vanishing as abruptly as they appeared. But they might also be snares thrown up by water specters and hungry ghosts anxious for a victim, warnings from Dragon Lords that ruled the sea. For the fish he saw were only glimpses of life at the surface, the thin upper layer of a strange, formidable world he could hardly guess at.

On his journey from the village to Hong Kong and the *S.S. Tanda,* he had also felt as if he were being thrust into a world purged of all that was familiar and real. His cousin and then his brother had been there to guide him, yet he had often thought during the first bewildering days and weeks and months that he would drown in his ignorance and misery. How was he going to make it through this alone?

"For civilized men, Hainan is a living hell, a tropical inferno of dark, malarial forests, wild tribesmen, and demon-haunted wilderness." The village schoolmaster's words, repeated so often, surfaced as clearly as if he were once again reciting the writings of officials banished to Hainan from the court in Peking. Their poetry was melancholy, their letters full of despair. But their dread of bugs and snakes made Lim and his friends scornful, and they laughed at the exiles' fears of forest goblins and evil spirits. Now Lim understood the exiles' alarm, their feelings of abandonment. At the same time, he wondered if his own terrors might be as exaggerated and unfounded as the exiles' had been. Nevertheless, he did not take down the bulwark.

Lim tied an eighth, ninth, and then a tenth knot in the lanyard. According to his calculations, the port authorities should have realized the *Benlomond* was overdue, and he stared impatiently at sea and sky.

His first trip at sea, he had marked off each day on a calendar hidden beneath his pillow, counting the days until the ship would return to Hong Kong and the possibility of a visit home. When his brother noticed, he said, "The essence of being a seaman is to live life in the present, to make both the past and the future disappear." Lim had never been successful at stopping his mind from drifting back to the past or looking to the future. But after the Japanese occupation of Hainan killed any hope of going home, he had stopped marking off the days and he had found that time did pass more easily.

Hoping it would have the same effect now, Lim stopped knotting the lanyard. The tenseness of waiting for rescue still hung over the raft like a thick dark cloud, but he found he was less fretful.

Looking for landfall now as well as a plane or ship, he methodically scanned the sea from starboard to port, up a few degrees, then back from port to starboard until he had covered all four sides of the raft. He repeated the process with the sky, then began again with the sea. At dusk, clouds low on the horizon sometimes looked like islands, and he studied their shapes, straining to uncover some proof that what he saw was more than mist. Could that thin white line against the blue horizon be distant breakers? Were those darker shadows palm trees fringing a beach? Surely that was the sound of rollers crashing against a rocky shore?

The infinite play of sun and clouds on water deceived over and over, so that all he could be absolutely certain about were his daily rations, a steady loss of weight, the eruption of painful spots and salt water boils on his feet, legs, and buttocks.

He lanced the boils with the jagged edge of a lid from a pemmican tin. Ripe, they broke easily, one after another, spewing out white and green matter, yellow pus, then clean red blood, and finally, a clear viscous liquid. But without any covering, he was unable to protect the sores from the constant action of salt water and the irritation of hard wooden planks, and the wounds refused to heal. Finally, Lim admitted he had as much to fear from his sores as the sea, and he knelt to take down the bulwark to use as bedding.

Reaching for the ties, he hesitated, remembering. More than a decade had passed since he had pitted Prince, his favorite cricket, against the village champion, but the memory remained like an ugly scar, a painful warning.

The boys said crickets would not fight unless they were kept in a jar for two or three days without food. But Lim had always pampered Prince, feeding it moistened tea leaves he begged from the owner of the tea stall in the market. The cricket had shown its gratitude with long shivery chirrups and peculiar little rattling songs it made with its wings, and Lim could not bear to starve it, even for a day.

When he put Prince into the ring, an old cooking pot, the cricket refused to fight. One of the boys tied a few rat whiskers to a little bamboo stick and taunted Prince and the other cricket until they were face to face. Still Prince would not fight. So the boy brushed Prince's big hind legs, irritating the cricket into a blind fury.

Lim remembered his surge of excitement when the crickets finally burst into action and the crowd of boys pressed hotly, cheering and cursing. Caught up in an electric silence as the fight intensified, the almost sexual release of collective breath at the finish, he had not seen the broken limbs that could not be mended, the last quivers of the pet he had betrayed for a wager. Only when Prince lay completely still and lifeless did he understand that gambling always demanded a loser as well as a winner, and as he dug his pet's shallow grave, he had sworn never to gamble again.

Fingers trembling, Lim fumbled with the first knot. He had broken his oath before to play mah jong and pai gow. But in those games, the stakes were never more than pennies. This time, the gamble was for his life.

CHAPTER NINE

The knotted ties proved troublesome, and by the time Lim finished taking down the bulwark, the raft was floating in a faint gleam of phosphorescence, the pale reflection of a misted moon. A sharp night breeze blew spray onto the deck, and he shivered as he clumsily folded the stiff, salt-encrusted canvas into six more or less equal portions and spread it out on the port deck, creating a seamless sleeping bag. A shroud?

He slid between the top folds and stretched out straight, arms at his side. Though coarse, the five bottom layers of canvas cushioned his bones and the cover kept him warm and dry. But the image of the canvas as a shroud and the narrow ledge a coffin kept him rigid and wide-eyed, listening for the slightest change in the wind or the slap of water against the raft.

The gentle, rhythmic swells that rocked Lim into a doze during the afternoons now kept him awake, and he stared up at the dusting of stars, the clouds that hung like the hoary locks of water specters eager to make a bid for freedom as soon as he sank into sleep. Finally, exhaustion overrode his fears. But even as his mind began the descent into sleep, his body twitched, and he jerked awake bathed in a sweat colder than the night dew.

The next morning he rose wearier than when he had laid down the night before. The same was true of the days that followed. Even when he did sleep, nightmares prevented rest. The dreams were always the same. He had fallen overboard, and though he paddled until his heart and lungs threatened to burst, the raft remained just out of reach. Eventually, his arms and legs grew so heavy they dragged him down, and he sank, still swimming, still trying to reach the raft.

Exhaustion drained Lim's already depleted strength, blurred his vision, and muddied his thinking. Because he was eating so little, he had almost no waste, a single bowel movement since the sinking. He told himself that if he could only have another bowel movement, he would make land. Or if he drank four dippers of water, it would be four days until rescue, if he drank three, he would have to wait only three. Or he would take a sight below the horizon, then lift his eyes slightly above and fix his eyes on a cloud, certain that if it rose, it would reveal a ship, if it did not move, it would be a land mass.

His moods rocketed, and he was either riding high on a belly full of hope or wallowing in deep despair. When there was absolutely no wind and the sea and raft were frozen like a painting, he would be depressed, afraid the raft would never make landfall. A whisper of wind or a quick, light patter of rain and his spirits would soar. Then every shadow on the horizon suddenly became a promise of land, every cloud a plane, every wrinkle in the sea the curl of foam from a ship's prow, every shooting star a ship's flare. But if the wind stirred up swells that hid the raft in troughs or it rained too hard or too long, his hopes would dissolve and he would cower in the well, afraid lightning might strike or he might be pitched out or washed overboard.

He had saved the rope ties. Yet he resisted putting up the bulwark. For his flesh was shrinking, the angles of his bones protruding further. More important, the sores dotting his body were finally healing and no new boils had appeared.

Gradually, the snatches of sleep grew longer. The nightmares receded. And though he remained apprehensive, he knew when he woke and found the sun instead of the moon that he had won.

There were other battles.

He followed the daily food and water allocation strictly at first. But during the long hot afternoons, he found it hard to curb his desire to quench his thirst when the tank held the water to satisfy it, and increasingly often, he drank his evening allotment long before dusk.

Though the food ration was also stringent, he rarely felt hungry. But he craved variety. Food became his main preoccupation and he understood why the exiles' writings that his teacher recited were so full of descriptions of past banquets. To former court officials, taro and yam, the staples for people on Hainan, must have seemed like hardtack did to him. Grinding his teeth back and forth, pulverizing the hardtack into gritty, tasteless crumbs, Lim imagined the fragrance of almonds crushed between smooth granite millstones, the sweet gruel made from the powder. Then, dipping his fingers into the pemmican one at a time and licking off the tasty brown coating, he imagined himself slurping up noodles strand by strand.

Just as he had anticipated special festival dinners as a child, he now mulled over the foods he would eat when he was rescued. Thoughts of molasses and sesame seed candy, taffy hard as rock and sticky enough to pull out teeth, twisted fritters, tart pickled vegetables, and the crisp skin of roasted chickens invaded his dreams, and he sometimes woke choking on his own saliva.

Rationing began to weigh on him. He tried drinking a little less and eating a little more on overcast days when food was more of an obsession, balancing it out by eating less and drinking more when it was hotter. That helped, and he tried other adjustments. A tin of milk, once opened, spoiled rapidly in the fierce heat, so he drank the whole tin all at once. When that gave him diarrhea that left him weak and dehydrated, he opened the tin at night. Then he kept it in a "cooler," a tin of seawater in the raft's well, during the heat of the day. The milk still spoiled, but not as quickly, and he was able to stretch it out for almost three days. By the second day his throat rebelled. Each clotted mouthful had to be swallowed several times before it stayed down, and for hours afterwards, sour milk coated his tongue and gums, fouling his mouth. But there was also no diarrhea.

To save water, he no longer made a soup out of the crushed hardtack. Instead he forced himself to eat it whole. He discovered that exposing the biscuits to the humid air softened them. Each morning, feeling like a village boy herding buffalo, he lay a few pieces out on the deck, watched them so they wouldn't fall. By night they were edible, and though they still required slow, continuous nibbling, he did not have to drink quite as much water to wash them down.

He kept himself relatively clean by washing after each rain. The canvas awning was not taut, and at the end of a shower it sagged with trapped water. If he was very careful, he could untie a corner and lift the awning off the pole without spilling any. Then, open mouthed, he tilted his face up and let the water drain down on his head, his shoulders, chest, and legs. He gargled. Using his knuckles and the palm of his hand, he scrubbed at the globs of grease and grime that covered his hot, salt-sticky skin. Without soap, the washes were not very effective. But for a little while after, his mouth felt less foul, his hair and skin less sweaty and sticky.

The initial, almost visible loss of flesh seemed to stop. Feeling the hollows between his ribs and above the bristles of beard, Lim guessed he was at least a stone lighter. The parts of his body that were normally clothed had tanned and his skin had toughened. His hair had grown so thick and full, it shaded his eyes from the glare during the day and cushioned his head like a pillow at night. Since he had stretched out to sleep rather than curling in a ball, he rarely experienced cramps in his legs, and the continuous balancing and bracing required to keep his footing when he walked the ledges provided a form of exercise.

Barnacles and bits of moss were growing on the sides of the raft, attracting fish that attracted other fish, and gelatinous masses bobbed like ghostly parachutes among them. Each morning, the golden blue fish that chased the flying fish rose up from the depths to swim parallel to the raft like a protective convoy. Sharks, the ugly torpedo fish, and shiny silver fish with yellow tails and short, muscular bodies appeared from time to time. And he saw flying fish almost every day, sometimes at night.

There were two-wing and four-wing types, he discovered. Some with beautiful color patterns. Others with only an oblique band extending across their forward wings. Some with lopsided tails. Others with flaplike whiskers extending downward from the tips of their lower jaws. But all of them could fly. In preparing to leave the water, they would drive very rapidly upward, and if their initial spurts were not sufficient to get underway, they would vibrate the long, lower lobes of their tails sideways, like outboard motors, until they were airborne. Holding their wings steady, they flew close to the water, going 150 feet and more in a matter of seconds. Watching them, Lim imagined himself skating across the surface as easily as they did until he reached home.

There were also tiny fish that swam alongside. Only an inch or two long, they nevertheless kept pace even when a stiff breeze was blowing, and Lim enjoyed their pretty colors as they swam about or nibbled the barnacles on the sides. Sometimes there would be a frantic churning as a large fish made a rush and the little fish dove for shelter under the raft. Always some failed to escape, and though Lim knew he was being childish, he occasionally interfered, leaning over and beating the attackers on their snouts with an oar.

The golden blue fish were his favorites. Some as small as three feet, a few as long as six, they liked to hide from the sun in the shadow cast by the raft, and like the torpedo fish, they sometimes bumped against the sides. But they were too playful to frighten. Watching them come and go, he came to recognize individuals from scars old and new, an open sore the size of a shilling, a torn fin, a hurt just above an eye. And he noticed they had different personalities. Some were timid, swimming away as soon as he lowered an oar into the water, while others were braver, staying close and bumping against the oar or rubbing against the side of the raft like itchy dogs trying to rid themselves of fleas.

Playing with them, Lim felt an easing of tension, and for a little while at least, he could forget that he had not once sighted a ship or plane since the ship had turned from him.

CHAPTER TEN

"One of the exiles," Lim's schoolmaster had lectured his students, "built a verandah onto his house. There he sat day after day, looking for a messenger to come with an official despatch ordering him home again. The messenger never came, and after he died, people called the lookout the balcony of endless days.

Hunkered down on the ledge, watching, waiting for rescue, Lim began to think of the raft as his balcony of endless days. Though he had long since stopped counting the days, he could not escape the moon. Already he had seen it grow round once, and now he was watching it rise larger and larger while the food and water supplies shrank smaller.

When he ran out of chocolate, sugar, and lime juice, he tried to tell himself the situation now was no different from when he was on the *Benlomond.* As a tramp, she had gone wherever there was cargo to be picked up, and not knowing how long it would be before she would be back in home port, the catering department was sometimes caught short of certain items available only in England. But of course this was different. Shortly after the first full moon he had eaten the last malted milk tablet. Two mornings previous, he had finished the last tin of milk. Now there was only a half box of hardtack, barely a fourth of a tin of pemmican, and one, at most two gallons of water. Not enough of anything to last this moon. So he ate and drank less, pretending that his gums were too sore for him to chew more than one piece of hardtack, that the rations were too monotonous and he was too tired to bother with them, that he wasn't hungry anyway. Anything, rather than admit he might consume the last of the supplies before rescue.

Despite the humidity that made breathing a chore, the sun's constant, malevolent glare sucked Lim dry. When there was no breeze and the temperature soared, he escaped the heat by lying in the well. Flat on his back, he could see nothing except the awning above, but it had been so long since the hum of engines had broken the silence that keeping a watch seemed almost as much of a charade as his fantasies. He realized it was important to stay alert and maintain self control. But daydreams of rescue, cigarettes, and real food provided a relief too sweet to give up, and he lapsed increasingly frequently into a lethargic drowsiness in which he was neither awake nor asleep.

His feet and ankles swelled from the long periods of sitting. His buttocks became sore from the constant friction of flesh against rough planks and canvas. And when he spent too much time in the well, his genitals swelled and the soles of his feet puckered and flaked. Yet it seemed to Lim he was watching it all happen to someone else.

While he had sugar and chocolate, sucking them had given him the lift he needed to carry him through the long afternoons, the hardest part of each day. Without them, he drummed his fingers on the deck, picked the split ends off his hair or sank into a dull doze.

Only the sight of rain clouds blotting the horizon quickened his pulse. Roused out of his apathy, he swiftly cleared away the hardtack, secured the bedding, and checked the ties holding the awning. Then, seething with nervous excitement, he watched the clouds spread like a black awning across the sky, the wind freshen, the sea darken and rise.

After the panic of the first squall, he had noticed that when the wind held steadily in one direction for a period of time, all the swells and surface waves would run in the same direction. Every sixth or seventh wave would be the big one that broke, and after that, everything would die down to a lull before building up to another breaker. Confident now of the raft's ability to ride the waves and his own to stay on board, he thrilled when the wind cracked the awning, straining at the ties, and massive swells pushed the raft into the depths of troughs and then up again. Only when the wind shifted direction did he tense, for the large swells would continue to run with the former wind direction while the surface waves would go in the new, and the raft would roll and pitch helplessly. Then he would remember stories of storms that smashed hull plates and fractured steam pipes, and he would cling to the planks, shouting prayers to Tien Hau.

During the last squall, when the raft became caught in the dark hollow of a trough, he saw a phantom ship rise out of the storm glowing with light. She approached silently on a collision course, so close he could clearly see the rotted decks, the skeletal crew, and the untended helm. Then, just as she was about to crash, a cry tore out of him, and she swung away leaving him shaken, unnerved.

Vaguely he sensed he was treading a thin line between madness and sanity. But like a pilot steering a ship through mined waters without a chart, he had no marked buoys to guide him.

Time was his biggest enemy. He had always worked with an economy of time and movement. But now his approach was slow, almost languid as he folded the canvas bedding and prepared his simple meals of hardtack, pemmican, and water.

Dimly he remembered a day during his ninth year when his mother had asked him to gather sticks and brush for the kitchen fire. The schoolmaster, a strict, humorless man, demanded perfect recitations, punishing any lapse, however small, with a sharp rap on the student's knuckles and wrists, and Lim, anxious to prepare his lessons well, complained that he had no time.

From her chair in the corner of the main room, his grandmother, her voice querulous, shrilled, "All it takes to kill a peasant is to keep him idle."

Old and frail, her mind often wandered and Lim, thinking she misunderstood, began to explain.

His mother, anxious to keep the peace, soothed, "Study is more important. I can..."

"How will the boy learn discipline if you insist on spoiling him?" his father snapped. His scowl, the slash of teeth gleaming between dark rectangle of moustache and beard, frightened Lim as badly as his teacher's switch, and he trembled when his father stamped so close their breath mingled. But his mother moved between them, fussing, distracting, enabling Lim to escape the chore, any real work until he signed articles as a learn boy on the *S.S. Tanda.*

He had run from the harsh conditions on the ship to the Wah Nam School in Hong Kong, and from school to the *Benlomond.* Here on the raft, the only escapes open to him were daydreams and sleep, and he came to crave them even more than cigarettes.

The early concerns that had prevented sleep meant nothing to him now. If there were no ships to rescue him during the day, there would be none to run him down at night. And if a storm surprised him and he rolled off the raft, would death and condemnation to eternal wandering be any worse than the agony of stewing day after endless day in this stifling cauldron of blazing skies and broken hopes?

Like an addict, he courted sleep, dreams of food and home, the ship that had come so close. In his dreams, the ship did not turn from him. Instead the officer with the binoculars lowered a Jacob's ladder and Lim was welcomed aboard. Clean and safe between fresh white sheets, he gratified starved nostrils, throat, and lungs with the keen pleasure of cigarettes....

Each time he woke to find himself still on the raft, the betrayal he had felt when the ship turned from him surged anew, and for a while, bitter waves of disappointment and anger would wash over him. Then he would pray to the sainted heroes and heroines, the Gods and Goddesses who live in the planets and constellations that brighten the night sky, begging them to use their influence on human destinies to bring him relief from the responsibilities and needs crushing his heart, his very will to live.

He thought most often of the men he had seen on the other raft. If they were drifting on the same currents as he was, shouldn't they be near? Yet he had not seen them since the first day. Did that mean that they had figured out how to sail for shore? He was sure it was possible to rig the canvas awning as a sail, but without any knowledge of winds and currents or even the direction in which land lay, he had no reason to try. The men on the raft could have pooled their knowledge and succeeded. Perhaps they had been picked up by a ship, the same ship that had turned from him. Or were they dying of starvation? After all, they had to share the same quantity of rations Lim had for himself alone. Could they have turned on each other, fighting, become cannibals?

The Ben Line must have acknowledged the loss of the *Benlomond* before the moon had reached her first fullness. By now they probably considered dead anyone not already rescued. Because of the Japanese occupation, they would not be able to notify his parents. But Gee Han who was serving in the Chinese army in India could have been notified, and he might have found a way to send word to their parents and Lim's betrothed.

The thought of her startled. Following custom, he had been betrothed as a child, not much more than a baby. A marriage broker had secured the arrangement between his parents and the girl's, and he had never seen her and would not see her until their wedding night. Months often went by without his remembering her existence, and he had not dreamed or thought of her once since being on the raft.

His brothers had been similarly betrothed, and before they left Hainan, their parents had made a wedding for Gee Hin, so there would be a daughter-in-law to take care of the cow, pigs, chickens, and light farm work that the boys would no longer be there to do. Then, when Gee Han turned twenty, their father ordered him home to marry. After the wedding, Gee Hin's wife was permitted to join her husband in Penang and the new bride assumed the chores. If the Japanese had not overrun Hainan, Lim would have gone home to marry as soon as he came of age. That way, Gee Han's wife could move to Hong Kong and make a home for her husband to return to when the *S.S. Tanda* docked there every few months, instead of having to wait long years before Gee Han could take a leave to go to the village.

Lim tried to picture his betrothed. Was she plump or thin? Was her skin pale or dark, coarse or smooth? Was her face pockmarked or clear, her hair shiny or dull? Was she good natured and generous or a vinegar bucket? He wondered if he was as faceless to her as she to him, whether she would seize the news of his death as an opportunity to marry someone else, or whether she would weep and comb her hair up into a widow's knot and refuse marriage until they came together in the spirit world.

Depressed by his thoughts of death, he reimagined his triumphant return to the village after the war, adding his betrothed to the people who came to hear him speak. She was short and plump, he decided, with clear pale skin, bright eyes and a cheerful smile, spirited yet willing, full of good humor and warmth, faithful, capable of giving him many sons.

All around the raft, silvery gleams of moonlight winked in the black water and phosphorescent fish made streaks and flashes, the shimmering glitter as dazzling as a traditional sequined wedding gown and beaded head dress.

Could this image be a sign?

Lim searched the night sky for an answer. But like the reverse of the moon, his future and his betrothed's were both invisible.

CHAPTER ELEVEN

The intensity of the sun on Lim's face warned him he had overslept. Afraid he would be late for setting up the officers' mess, he bolted upright, swung his legs over the side of the bunk. Water sloshed through the slats of the well, his toes, and he felt a sickening blow between his chest and the pit of his belly.

He no longer expected rescue. Yet he had not stopped believing it would come and his head jerked up automatically to search sea and sky. But his eyes remained sealed, reluctant to confront the almost certain emptiness.

He plowed his fingers through his thickly matted hair, showering his shoulders and lap with powdery salt. There had been a brief shower during the night and the sag in the middle of the awning probably still held enough water to allow the cleansing of sleep from eyes, the run of damp fingers through tangled hair and beard, a gargle. But the knots securing the canvas had become crusted with salt, making them difficult to untie, and he didn't have the patience to work them loose.

Leaning back against his elbows, he squinted speculatively at the awning. Once or twice during a heavy rain squall, he had pressed the flat end of an oar against the center of the awning so the water collected could spill over the edge, easing the stress on the canvas. He ran furry tongue around coated teeth and swallowed thickly. Perhaps he could do the same thing now, tilt the canvas with the oar and drain the water down into a can.

Manipulating the puddle of water towards the edge just above the deck was trickier than Lim anticipated. But he could not hope to catch the water in a tin unless he stood on a ledge, and he had to climb the two-and-a-half feet from the well while holding the oar against the canvas, tilting it just enough to keep the water flowing in the direction desired, yet not so much that it would reach the edge before he and the tin did.

On his first attempts the water kept running back to the center. Then, overcompensating, he raised the oar too high and lost a dribble of water over the edge before he could get to it. Annoyed but too involved in the challenge to give it up, he practiced climbing up onto the ledge until he could do it smoothly.

Now oar and awning wobbled only slightly as he stepped up onto the ledge. He took one careful step towards the edge, felt his foot tangle in the bedding he had pushed aside earlier. Cursing, he kicked the canvas out of the way bit by bit, trying not to disturb the delicate balance of oar and awning, then continued his slow progression to the edge.

He lifted the tin up in readiness, bringing it just ahead of the tip of the oar and a few inches lower so that the water would drain directly into the tin. To make the reach less awkward, he turned slightly and felt one foot, then both feet step into air.

The sea rose greedily, the water sucking him down just as it had when the *Benlomond* sank. But this time, he had no life jacket. Panicking, he plunged deeper, gulped more water.... Then, inexplicably, he was rising as though lifted by unseen, unknown hands, breaking the surface, spluttering and coughing.

The raft was not far, no more than a yard or two, the water smooth. But images of sharks, water specters, and vagrant ghosts bound Lim in a stranglehold that paralyzed his arms and legs, and he sank again, plummeting like a stone.

Images from his dreams flashed, meshed with the present. He was swimming, struggling to reach the raft, his arms and legs growing heavy, dragging him down. Memories and desires swirled and he wondered if he were experiencing the replay of life that people said came before death.

But he wanted to live, not die.

He kicked and thrashed his arms, clawing wildly at water, the oar, and air.

Suddenly, his fingers found the lifeline that becketed the raft.

Gasping, he clung to it. Barnacles scratched. His skin crawled with goosebumps, and he could not stop shaking. He knew he could not pull himself back on board unless he got hold of the lanyard on the opposite side of the raft. But he clutched the lifeline, terrified that he would lose the raft if he let go.

Little fish swam close, brushing against his limbs and he felt an awful nibbling. Absurdly frightened, he splashed with his legs, his elbows, shouting, turning the water into a boil, wasting energy he did not have. But he could not stop himself until all the fish had scattered, diving under the raft, swimming rapidly away in all directions.

Slowly, painfully, he loosened his right hand just enough to slide it a few inches across the lifeline then gripped hard. The intense concentration and effort required to uncurl his fingers shocked Lim, adding to his fears. But he pushed on, unlocking his other fingers, moving them down so both fists clasped the rope side by side. Then he slackened his hold and moved his right arm a few more inches, tightened the fingers back into an iron grip, and released his other hand, bringing it close.

When he finally reached the lanyard, he clasped it to his chest for a moment of victory. Then he wearily wound the knotted rope around both fists and tried to scramble up the three feet between water and deck.

The distance was the same as from well to ledge. But there were no planks to step up from and the side was rough with barnacles. He grunted, shifted positions, tried again. But cramps made his arms and legs difficult to control.

He grappled with different approaches, pitting his will against weakened muscles, exhaustion, and fear.

And then, without warning, he lost his grip on the lanyard and was sliding back into the water.

"No."

As the cry tore out of Lim, his fingers bumped against the knots in the lanyard, slowing his fall, and he regained his hold.

His every breath rasping short and ragged, he fought to regain the hard-won inches he had lost.

Air chilled his emerging body.

Rope, barnacles, metal, and then the hard edges of rough decking scraped his flesh raw. His arms shot out and he released the rope, jabbed his fingers between the planks, wedging them in.

Suspended between raft and water, Lim felt like a beast hung up for slaughter, completely drained. A steel band bound his chest. Scythes slashed his tendons. But with one last burst of effort he dragged himself, heaving and panting, over the side and tumbled into the well.

The position of the sun and the swelling of his feet told Lim he had been in the well for hours. Salt water stung his lacerations. Strained muscles ached. But the pain seemed remote, and he surveyed the scratches and bruises darkening his skin as dispassionately as if his body belonged to someone else.

Abruptly he grasped his head with both hands and shook it impatiently, spraying water in every direction. Had he learned nothing from his fall? Even now, only a few biscuits, a sprinkling of pemmican, and two or three pints of water separated him from death, and he was still trying to hide like a child, to pretend it was not happening.

But what else could he do?

"You cannot change the will of Heaven." Wasn't that what his mother said?

He had tried once with a chick when he was a boy. For three weeks he had checked the five eggs nestled under their hen every time he went to feed her. Then one morning there was only one egg. The rest had become hopping balls of fuzzy yellow down. Squatting to play with them, he saw the remaining egg was cracked, heard the chick pecking weakly within. He reached for it. Immediately, the hen attacked, pecking Lim and the chick struggling inside the half broken shell.

Yelping more from shock than pain, Lim dropped the egg back into the nest of rice straw.

"You must not interfere," his mother scolded from the doorway.

"But this last chick can't get out of its shell."

His mother nodded. "Then it's too weak to live. The hen knows this, that's why she wants you to leave it alone."

"We can't just watch it die."

"Neither can we change Heaven's will."

Though he was only eight or nine, Lim had already learned it was useless to argue with his mother once she invoked Heaven. But as soon as she left, he slipped inside, took her scissors from her sewing box, slyly rolled the egg away from the hen, and carefully cut away the shell.

For a long time, the only sign of life was a faint quivering beneath plastered-wet down. Then slowly the chick struggled to its feet and tottered around Lim, its tiny beak tapping ticklish caresses on the finger he extended.

Within days, the only difference marking this chick from the others was the eye blinded by the hen's attack. And its devotion to Lim.

For more than a year, no one in the village saw one without the other. Then the morning of the mid-autumn festival it failed to answer Lim's call. He searched the house, the courtyard, the village square, the river bank, the fields, refusing to give up until darkness forced him home.

The aroma of cooked chicken greeted him.

"One Eye could not lay eggs," his mother explained. "It was a useless ricebowl."

According to his mother, Lim had simply delayed Heaven's will by cutting open the chick's shell. And each time an animal or child sickened, a crop failed, or a dream died, she had repeated, "You cannot change the will of Heaven," until it became a truth he accepted without question.

But now he also remembered the furious activity with which she met each new trouble. The potions she brewed, the incense she burned, the prayers she muttered, the new dreams she whispered before the ashes of the old grew cold. Even the stories she told of legendary heroes struggling against terrible dangers and powerful enemies belied her apparent acceptance of Heaven's will.

After the *Benlomond* sank, he had not simply floated, waiting wishfully for Heaven to intervene; he had swum until he found the raft. And since then he had kept a watch, sent off signals, calculated rations, made himself bedding.... Now he must find a way to provide himself with food and drink.

He decided to tackle the water problem first.

Hardly a day passed without rain. Nevertheless, it was undependable. The squalls, usually lasting fewer than five to ten minutes, could bring down torrents that flattened swells less than a half mile away while the sky directly above remained a dazzling, cloudless blue. And the rain that did hit was often no heavier than a mountain mist. Or a heavy downpour could be followed by days of fierce humidity unrelieved by even a sprinkle. Moreover, rain was coming less frequently and falling in smaller quantities, and he worried that the weather here might be the same as on Hainan. Both were in the tropics, so it was possible. But that would mean the rainy season had already climaxed and he was entering a dry spell. He shuddered. Any attempt to endure this cruel sun without a reliable water supply would mean certain death.

He forced his shudder into a determined shrug. Even if there were a drought, he could have all the water he needed. After all, the raft had a water tank, one that held 10 gallons, enough water to carry him up to now, enough to carry him through a dry period lasting two moons. All he had to do was to figure out how to fill it.

The canvas awning trapped rain, but the water he took from it for washing and gargling was too salty to drink. To turn the awning into an effective catchment area, he would have to wash it as clean of salt as possible at the beginning of each shower and make it easily accessible for bailing into the water tank. But the clouds usually burst without warning, and the showers were generally too brief to allow time for taking down the canvas, washing, then putting it back up; and he would never risk another attempt with oar and tin.

Chewing his lips thoughtfully, he studied the awning. Trapped water from heavy showers had strained the fabric. With time and wear, the slight sag in the center would certainly worsen and the canvas might split.

Wasn't that why houses were built with roofs that sloped into gutters? Of course! That was the solution!

Lim rose stiffly, climbed onto a ledge. Standing made him dizzy, fully aware of his exhaustion, and he wondered if he should wait a day before trying out his plan. Easing himself back into the well, a splinter snagged under a fingernail. He sat down on the ledge and plucked it out with his teeth.

He examined his nails critically. Most of his nails had snapped and broken during his scramble back onto the raft. But he must chew smooth the ragged edges or they would snag and rip when he untied the awning. Gnawing, he considered his plan for a water catchment. He might have to wait days before it rained and he could try it out. By then there would be no water left in the tank, and if the plan did not work and he had to try another....

He could not risk delaying even a day, he decided. But fearful of another fall, he tied the lanyard around an ankle before making any attempt to take down the awning. Wrapping one leg and an arm around a corner post, he leaned his weight against it, wincing as rough wood scratched against sores, and fumbled with the knots.

Pulled tight by the wind, they resisted. His fingers, sore from the morning's struggles, were clumsy. Sweat dripped down his face, his back and chest. His upstretched arms ached. Feeling faint, he dropped back into the well to rest, then tried again.

Before the knot finally loosened, he had to rest twice more, and the ties on the opposite pole were equally difficult. But he was determined to finish, to provide the reassurance he needed even more than rest.

In the half-light of dusk he knelt and held the loosened ends of the awning at an angle, looping up the lower corners to form a shallow depression where rain water could collect. Then he tied the canvas into position about a foot from the base of each pole, forming the catchment he needed.

A gentle evening breeze riffled the canopy. If it freshened into a wind, it could turn the awning into a sail that would speed the raft's drift and pull at the makeshift ties. Depending on its direction and strength, the wind could even invert the shallow depression in the canvas, spilling out any water it held, preventing the collection of any more. The pitched awning also cut by half the tiny area where he could stand upright and walk, and it meant he could not see either sea or sky on the leeward side. But the slope would allow rain to easily, almost naturally, wash the canvas free of salt. And the catchment was low enough to make bailing into the water tank swift, so the canvas should not have to bear undue stress.

That was the plan. Now he needed rain to test it.

CHAPTER TWELVE

There was no question his food would be fish. The problem was how to catch them. At home he had used a hook and line his father had made for him. He remembered watching his father cut a piece of bamboo and several stems of reeds, each piece just slightly smaller than the one before, then fitting them together into a flexible rod. For the line, his father had braided together sixteen plies of raw silk from the cocoons spun by the wild silk worms that lived in the sweet gum tree near the temple. The hook was hammered out of an old tin earring Lim had found on the path to the market years before. His father attached a few bits of lead as weights and a float made with sections of bird quills.

Squatting on a broad, flat stone wedged into the muddy river bank, Lim's father threaded the hook with part of an earthworm. "Always use what you have," he instructed. "The young men in the villages where I taught martial arts had no money for fancy swords or lances, so I taught them to fight with what they did have: hoes, shovels, and sticks."

Even when asked, his father rarely talked about those times, and Lim leaned forward, excited, anxious to hear more. But his father gave him the baited rod without saying anything further. Feeling cheated, crushed by unarticulated questions and vague, anxious stirrings, Lim cast blindly. But as the hook touched water, he felt an unexpected, almost magical easing of tension.

It had been the same whenever he fished. Always the simple act of holding a fishing line soothed disconnected thoughts and sensations as effortlessly as the river smoothed jagged rocks. And though nothing really changed, the peace stayed with him like a talisman against daily irritations, disappointments, and misunderstandings. For a while.

He thought of his mother reaching for her sewing whenever she was troubled, the way the furrows creasing her forehead gradually disappeared as she stitched. And his father. Weren't his trips to the shore to buy fish always preceded by explosions of unexplained anger, just as they were then followed by a relaxed good humor that permeated the entire family? He remembered how his sister-in-law begged permission to go and gather fuel when his mother's demands became excessive. The letters and poems the exiles had written. All of them had sought and found escape.

But now fishing would be for more than release. It would be his only means to obtain food.

Lim picked at the knots he had made in the lanyard to mark off the days. On board ship, deckhands used a pointed steel tool for opening strands of rope that had to be spliced. He didn't have one, but this rope was not a thick hawser, and he was sure he could somehow take it apart and make a fishing line out of the strands. Yet he was reluctant to begin, for once the lanyard was gone, he would have nothing to help him back onto the raft should he fall overboard again.

The night before, lying rigid, his fingers gripping the edges of the decking, he had considered wrapping his canvas bedding back around the raft. Then there would be no chance of his falling overboard. But he would also lose his protection against the hard decking and the chill night wind. He had argued with himself through a long sleepless night, and now he ran a hand thoughtfully over the canvas bedding and the lanyard, unsure what he should do with either.

Like a passing frieze, he saw fishermen, their sampans bright as fireflies in the night-dark sea, trawling for fish; others crouched on special bamboo rafts, waiting until the fish swarmed thick as farmers on market day, then catching them in encircling nets.... Could he make a net?

Canvas was too coarse, but the burlap around the lime juice bottle might work. He threw open the food tank where he kept the empty tins and boxes and pulled out the bottle and a pemmican tin lid. Carefully, he scraped the jagged edge of the lid down the side of the bottle, slitting the coarsely woven fabric. When he pressed down hard, the jagged tips sawing through the burlap bent, but the lid itself did not. He could beat down the serrated edges with the heavy water tank key and cut off the curved tip of the oval to make a knife. A knife he would need to cut up the fish he caught. Lim set the lid down. There would be no fish to cut unless he found something to catch them with, and the scrap of burlap was too small.

Crouching stiffly, he dipped an arm into the sea to scoop up salt water to wash out his scratches. A small school of golden fish darted towards him. There were so many fish, why couldn't he just grab one? His arm shot through the water. Rough scales grazed his palm. Seizing the fish sliding past his fingers, he grasped a surge of water, emptiness.

Feeling foolish, he delved back into the food tank. Lifetime habits of frugality had prevented him from throwing anything away, but the expectation of finding something useful in this clutter seemed absurd. He organized the rusted bits of metal, empty tins, and boxes into neat piles within the tank, set the last of his rations carefully on top, shoved the empty jar and bottle into a corner, the torch beside them.

Pushing it into place, he accidentally triggered the switch. The glow reminded Lim of his first nights on the raft when he had turned on the torch at every imagined sound, and flying fish, attracted by the light, had leaped blindly onto the deck: If he caught fish with the light from the torch, then he could keep the lanyard intact and still have food!

Whistling softly, he began work on the knife. Pressing down the jagged edges did not require strength. But the vicious barbs did demand his careful attention. Yet he could not push back the questions that crowded the edges of his concentration. Was he likely to fall off the raft again? Should he put up the canvas or keep it for bedding?

When he dipped for water, the measure scraped the bottom of the tank. Would it rain before he ran out? He glanced up at the sky. The western horizon was pale with ashen clouds. Would those clouds darken, the gentle breeze rippling the water gather force and stiffen into a wind that would bring rain? Or would the clouds thin, the breeze wither and die? And when it did rain, would the awning work as a catchment?

Though he had used the torch frequently at night for probably more than half a moon, only four or five fish had flown onto the raft. At that rate, would there be enough meat to keep him alive?

That night Lim tied the lanyard around an ankle, then squatted on the ledge and turned on the torch, throwing a weak beam on the water about five feet from the raft. Was it the bright glow of the three-quarter moon that made the torch light seem pale or were the batteries wearing down? Or were the connections simply damp?

He unscrewed the handle. The batteries slid out and he rubbed them with the burlap, put them back, and pushed the switch. The light flickered dimly. He jiggled the batteries out again. The coil of wire that held them in place sprang onto the deck. He grabbed it, barely saving it from the sea, quickly stuffed it back into the safety of the handle.

About to screw the top back on, he hesitated, pulled the spring out and gazed thoughtfully at the curl of wire cupped in the palms of his hands. He smiled. It did not matter that the torch would not work for catching fish. A few twists, some fine honing of the point, and the spring would be a perfect hook.

But a hook required a line, taking apart the lanyard looped around his ankle.

His smile faded. He could have food. Or he could have a safety line. He could not have both.

It took almost a full day to unravel and rebraid the lanyard.

As the strands of hemp slowly spread across his lap, Lim planned. The fishing line would be the same length as the lanyard, but only a fraction of the thickness. With the rest of the hemp, he would make a "handle" for the knife. The beaten-down edges of the pemmican tin lid were still sharp enough to nick his hands, and it was awkward to hold. But a generous wrapping of hemp would make it safe to use and give it a solid grip. He should also braid ties that could be attached to the corner poles so the knife and fishing tackle would be readily available for use, yet safe. And he should keep part of the hemp for mending, making things he might not now anticipate needing.

At first, the lines Lim wove were loose and uneven. Unraveling and replaiting the strands of hemp until his fingers finally fell into an awkward rhythm, he did not finish braiding the fishing line, a handle for the knife, and the ties for both until long after the moon rose. Too excited to sleep, he extracted the spring from the torch and twisted it into a hook, then filed the point against the metal water tank key, honing it to needle sharpness.

The slope of the canvas awning hid the moon sinking towards the horizon, but there was just enough light to locate the box of hardtack at the top of the food tank. He was not hungry; the prospect of hardtack was unappetizing; and there were so few pieces left that the temptation was to save them all. But if he did not eat, he would not have the strength necessary to scrub the canvas and bail water when it rained or to pull in his catch.

Crushed hardtack plastered his gums and teeth. Peeling off the hardening paste with his tongue, balling it into a lump and forcing himself to swallow, he imagined the fish he would be eating tomorrow, and when he finally slept, he dreamed of pearly slivers of meat sliding easily down his throat.

CHAPTER THIRTEEN

Rain stung Lim's face, puncturing warm dreams with wet pinpricks of cold. Annoyed, he burrowed deeper into the canvas bedding. But drops pesky as insistent flies crawled down his neck and chest, chilling.

He leaped up to check the awning. Without moonlight, he could not see, but he could hear the rain drumming on canvas, and he could feel the water cascading into the trough, splashing over the rim. He scooped some into cupped palms, gulped greedily, spat. The water might as well be from the sea, it was so salty!

Deeply disappointed, Lim dropped into the well to figure out his next step. From the feel of the raft, the slap of waves against the sides and the wash of water across his feet, he knew the swells were not high and they were rising and falling in an even rhythm. Neither was the wind tugging at the rope ties strong. But mindful that he no longer had a lanyard either to secure him or to help pull him back on board if he should slip and fall, he was wary of climbing onto the outside edge of the deck, preferring to wait for the rain to wash the awning clean of salt. At the same time he worried that he could not afford the wait. There had been no rain for two days, and though he had been miserly with his water ration, there was barely enough left in the tank to get him through one more stifling afternoon. What if this squall didn't last long enough for him to collect fresh water, and he had to wait another two days for the next shower?

Clinging to the corner pole, Lim climbed onto the ledge and stepped over the lowered corner of the awning to face the slanted canvas squarely. Then, toes gripping the wood slats, he began scrubbing the canvas with his right fist, working from the farthest, highest edge down to the curve of canvas just below his feet.

Rain pelted him, dissolving the salt scaling his flesh, his hair and beard. Lightning crackled and a loud drum-roll of thunder followed. Fearful the squall might intensify, he crawled back into the well, slid his arms below the curve of the canvas and pushed up, spilling out all the salt-tainted water. Then he opened the food tank to get a tin for bailing.

In the dark, the neat piles of tins, boxes, and scrap metal became a dangerous tangle. He cursed angrily at the sharp edges, his lack of planning. Finally he found one. He scooped up freshly collected rain from the canvas trough, sipped. Better, but the taste of salt remained distinct.

Twice more he spilled water out of the awning before recognizing that he was hoping for a freshness that was impossible. He opened the water tank, scooped water from the canvas catchment into the tin and poured it into the tank.

Over and over he scooped and poured, scooped and poured.

The muscles he had strained during the scramble back onto the raft ached.

The wind dropped.

The sea calmed.

The drumming of rain on canvas became a light pitter-patter, the water sliding down into the trough not much more than a trickle. But he continued to bail until the rain stopped entirely and the catchment contained only a trace of dampness steaming in the pale warmth of the rising sun.

The water he had saved filled a little less than one-fifth of the tank, about two gallons. Next time he would do better. There would be a smaller salt buildup to wash off, and as soon as he saw potential rain clouds gathering on the horizon, he would sprinkle the catchment with seawater. That should dissolve most of the salt. Then, when the rain began, he could use the burlap, which was more abrasive than his fists, to scrub off the final film of salt. And he would make hemp ties for the piece of burlap and the bailing tin so they could be hung on a pole where they would always be within reach. But first he would try out his hook and line.

As always after a squall, there were fewer fish, and there were no large ones at all. A foot-long bright green fish with a forklike tail sparkled like an emerald among a scattering of smaller silvery blue, violet, and dull brown ones. Which should he try for?

Since his hook was small, he had made a short line. That way he could pull it in quickly if a large fish threatened to bite. But beyond that he had no idea what other safeguards he should take. Or what he could use for bait. At home he had used worms or young frogs. But he had heard of fishermen who used dough. If he wadded some pemmican up into a ball, wouldn't that be the same?

Apparently not. Almost as soon as the hook touched water, the ball of pemmican disintegrated and little fish surfaced and gulped the specks like pets in a tropical aquarium. He tried to force the hook into a broken piece of hardtack, but the point began to bend. Soaking the hardtack made it soft enough for the hook to pierce, too soft to hold up in the sea for long, and again small fish darted after the loosened crumbs, gobbling.

Undaunted, Lim lowered the hook into the sea without bait. Keung Tai Gung, the great Prime Minister of the Chou Dynasty, had fished without bait, declaring the fish, if they were willing, would come to him. And they had. So too would they come to Lim's hook.

A few circled it. He jiggled the line. The silver curl of metal glimmered, enticing. One of the brownish fish swam close. But just as the point of the hook neared its tiny mouth, it flicked its tail and darted away. Turning on its side, it repeatedly swam close, but never quite close enough.

He worked the hook slowly towards a small school traveling parallel to the raft. The little fish dove out of sight as though the hook were a big fish about to attack. Waiting for them to reappear, Lim wondered how long Keung Tai Gung had waited before snagging a fish on his empty hook, what he would do if these fish were not willing to come to him.

He held the line still. When that produced no results, he tried playing it. The rough fibers bit into the nicks and cuts scarring his hands, snagging scabs, worrying new sores, and still nothing tugged at the line. At home he had sometimes rested his rod on a forked branch stuck in the river bank, and he debated attaching the line to the oar which he could sit on, giving his hands a rest.

He flexed his stiff fingers, frowned worriedly at the cuts made by the barnacles. They seemed to be taking longer to heal than previous scratches and a few were beginning to fester. Were barnacles poisonous? Impossible. Barnacles were what the fish dove below the raft to feed on.... He laughed out loud, the sound shattering the silence, frightening the fish below. Barnacles. Bait! He was sitting on top of bait!

Still chuckling, he wound in his line, took down his knife and pried loose a barnacle from just below the water line. He broke the shell with the water tank key, pierced the lump of flesh with the hook, and dropped the line over the side.

For a while the fish avoided it. But the succulent morsel was too sweet to ignore forever. There were a few bubbles near the bait. He felt a downward pull, watched one of the small, brownish fish nibble all the meat without touching the hook. Disgusted, Lim wound in the line, rebaited it, and recast, this time throwing down the remaining bits and pieces of broken shell and meat as well. Little fish swarmed over the unexpected shower of tidbits.

There was a tug at the hook. With an exultant yank, Lim pulled in the line, almost dropping it when the fish's spine shot out and it gave an unexpected grunt. Grabbing the fish by its tail, Lim slammed it against the deck, knocking it senseless. He worked loose the hook, rinsed his tackle, and lashed it to the corner pole, then examined his catch.

Though brown in the water, the fish now seemed colorless, and he was disappointed to see that almost half of its nine-inch length was taken up by its head. Since it was quite a flat fish, there would be very little meat. He decided to saw off the head but leave the tail so he could hold it while scaling and cleaning what was left.

The skin, free of scales, remained an unappetizing gray. He peeled off a corner of skin with his knife and cut a small wedge of meat. On his palm, the lump of pinkish flesh was not at all the delicate, pearl white sliver he had imagined the night before. He sniffed it cautiously. His nose wrinkled at the curious odor of ammonia, and though he knew it was foolish, he felt an overpowering urge to wash it in the sea.

He closed his eyes instead. Further examination was pointless. There was fish. Or there was nothing. And while Gods might live well enough on air, he was a man, and a man required food.

As though he could shut out taste and smell along with sight, Lim kept his eyes closed as he bit into the rubbery lump. He forced his teeth to grind back and forth. The pungent taste made him wonder what the fish had eaten besides moss, barnacles, and other shelled creatures. Seaweed, perhaps. Or refuse from ships. The bodies of his dead shipmates.

Lim fought the image, the impulse to spit out the mess in his mouth. This fish had eaten no differently than the hundreds of fish he had consumed in the past and enjoyed, only they had been cooked, flavored with ginger, garlic, green onions, and cilantro, steamed until their flesh fell apart at the touch of a chopstick. The bit of fish he was chewing was raw.

Would he become ill from eating raw meat? Perhaps even poisoned? Nonsense. In Japan he had been in restaurants that served uncooked fish. It was simply a matter of getting used to it.

He thought of the first meal he had actually tried to eat on the *S.S. Tanda*, the older steward who had laughed when he saw Lim poking suspiciously at the gooey mess on the plate. "Just remember," he had said. "So long as its back faces Heaven, it's edible."

But he could not swallow. His throat contracted so it refused even saliva and a harsh pricking spread up through his nostrils. If he did not empty his mouth, he would not be able to breathe.

Leaning over the side, he spat. Tiny fish rushed to nibble the foul bits of matter. Shuddering, Lim wrenched open the water tank, gargled furiously, then drank. One dipperful. Two. Three. A fourth. But he could not rid his mouth of the sour, fetid taste.

He looked at the hook and line. The ocean empty of ships. The sky without the shadow of a plane. The headless fish on the deck.

Hardtack had made him choke, yet he ate it. Out of necessity. To keep up his strength. To live. Wasn't that why beggars ate refuse, even mud and grass? Deliberately, Lim reached for his knife and gutted the fish. Part of a liver, or was it the heart, slid through the slats of planking, disappeared. Along with it sank Lim's resolve. Nevertheless, he continued to work, prying loose the bone, for he knew resolve would return with hunger. Not today. Not tomorrow. He had enough hardtack to see him through that long. But after that. Perhaps not immediately. But eventually, when need overcame all other considerations, he would eat.

He stopped in mid-cut. Wouldn't the fish be spoiled by then? Already the smell was getting stronger. How long before the reek of death became the stench of decay?

If only he had salt and wicker racks, he could preserve the fish like his father did. But he did have salt. A whole ocean of salt! As for racks, they were only used when large quantities of fish were being dried. For household use, his mother and other housewives strung a loop of twine through each fish tail, then hung the fish from a bamboo pole. That was what he would do. String hemp between the corner poles and hang the fish he caught by their tails. While they dried, the salt that crystallized on the canvas awning and his own body would crystallize on them too! Shooting both fists high above his head, Lim shouted his victory to Heaven.

CHAPTER FOURTEEN

To give the drying fish the full force of the sun and the maximum circulation of air, Lim strung two lines parallel to the slope of the awning. He looped a bit of hemp through the tail of the fish he had caught and tied it to a line. Then he readied the food tank for storing his new rations, stowing the empty tins, boxes, bottle, and torch in the two compartments and scrubbing the tank absolutely clean of rust.

Three or four times during the afternoon and the following morning, he checked the fish on the line to make sure its strong odor was the fragrance of salting and drying, not the stink of decay. He caught seven more little fish, cleaned and hung them on the lines. Then he braided a string for the bailing tin and three dozen more ties to loop through the tails of additional fish after he caught them.

By mid-afternoon, the fierce heat of the sun and the heavy concentration of salt in the atmosphere seemed to have completed the curing process. Like jerky, the dried fish was a fraction of the size and weight of the fresh. The meat had darkened, and it looked nothing like the raw fish Lim had chewed the day before. But memory of the foul taste lingered, the mere thought of the squishy lump sending all his senses into frantic revolt, and his initial nibble was cautious, more a tentative peck than a real bite.

He was pleasantly surprised. The texture was chewy, the flavor mild. A half inch of his mother's salt fish was enough to spice up a large bowl of plain congee. This was much blander, tasting more like the broiled fish the British seemed to favor. When forced to eat it as a steward, he had not cared for the tepid, fishy taste, but after almost two moons of little more than hardtack, he found the flavor close to delicious.

Not all the fish would take the hook and line. And of those that would, many were unsuitable. Some were too small. Others were too large. And some, like those with spiked spines or bellies that puffed up like balloons when touched, he avoided because other fish did. To wait for the right moment and the right fish required patience combined with an ability to strike instantly when the moment arrived.

Because they were greedy, the brownish fish were the easiest to catch. But their bony scales and sharp fins and teeth cut Lim's fingers and they gave so little meat that it took over twenty fish to make a barely adequate meal. A longer, silvery fish was fleshier, its scales softer, and it was apparently toothless. But its mouth was so tiny Lim was often tricked into pulling in the line before it was fully hooked, losing the fish and scaring away others around it. The green and the blue-striped fish were either too nervous or too clever to be caught, and after a few days even the brownish ones became more cautious.

While the moon shone round and bright, flying fish, apparently attracted by the sloped awning's white gleam, sometimes flew into the canvas, leaving one or two trapped in the trough. Though less than a foot long, their bodies were rounder, their heads not as disproportionately large as the fish Lim caught, so they provided twice as much meat. But when the full moon passed a few nights later, he had to again make do with what he could catch himself.

Though tension often cramped the muscles in Lim's neck and shoulders, he did not really mind the challenge; and after one-and-a-half moons of doing little more than sitting and waiting, he welcomed the seemingly endless chores that now filled every moment of daylight. Pulling in his catch, cutting and cleaning, he thought of his mother and sister-in-law who passed all their days in mundane household tasks. Did they also find the routine a comforting ritual, the need to provide a reason for rising at dawn? Did they feel the same sense of achievement at the end of each day?

The first time it rained, he wrestled with the tiny knots that held up each piece of fish, then realized he could get them all down simply by taking in both lines. Anxious to finish washing the canvas and save as much clean water as possible, he carelessly laid the fish on the deck where they became splashed during the bailing, and by the time the rain passed, the fish hung in limp, damp strips that disintegrated into slimy messes when touched. He did not make that mistake again. But when he tried hiding them in the food tank, the fresh fish spoiled the dry. Now, as soon as dark clouds gathered, Lim retied the lines of drying fish under the high side of the awning where they were sheltered from the worst of the rain and the bailing.

He braided a longer string for his knife and wore it around his neck when he fished so that he could immediately scale, cut, and remove the guts and backbone from his catch. Piles of gray scales ridged the slats of wood where he rubbed the edge of his knife clean. The rank little piles and the drops of fish blood stank so badly in the heat that he had to scrub the deck two or three times in a single morning, and his hands became swollen and cracked from the cutting and cleaning.

For reasons he could not fathom, the fish never bit after the sun rose to its peak, and when the sea was lumpy, they seemed to vanish entirely. He had to be careful to keep the fishing line from rubbing against the raft so it would not wear itself out, and he had to maintain a sharp watch for passing shadows and schools which warned of larger fish that might break his tackle.

Soon the effort required to catch and dry four or five dozen fish a day, then clean and sharpen his tackle became exhausting. He was impatient when rain fell and interrupted his cycle of fishing and drying, resentful of the extra burden that bailing added. But if two or three days passed without a shower, he became anxious.

To save time and energy, he used pieces of liver and heart for bait instead of barnacles. And when he saw how attracted the fish were to blood, he tossed the entrails and heads overboard in batches. Then, as the fish swarmed, he scooped up handfuls of the unwary. Sometimes, when his fingers became too sore to hold the line, he dangled an intestine over the side. But if he did not pull it in fast enough after a fish began to swallow, the fish would bite through it and escape.

The erratic movement of the shiny hook, the intestines, fish, and blood attracted a new rush of torpedo fish and sharks. The torpedo fish's jutting lower jaws, fang-like teeth, and mighty leaps and the sharks' wide, cruel mouths and thrashing tails frightened Lim; and he worried that other fish might also be lurking below, too far down for him to see, but close enough to attack. Worse, the sharks scared away the smaller fish on which he depended, making it increasingly difficult for him to catch even the minimum he needed.

Getting started in the morning took longer and longer, and by dusk, his head rolled limp against his chest and sleep seemed more urgent than eating the fish he had toiled to catch. Yet when he finally crawled beneath his canvas bedding, memories of One Eye, the chick he had tried to save as a boy, prevented sleep. Were his struggles to stay alive now just as futile?

A memory, long buried, surfaced: Because his mother's feet had been bound in childhood, Lim's father carried the heavy wooden buckets of water for household use from the village well, though it was a woman's chore. Yet she plodded eight li to visit her mother each month and carried Lim as well. Always when they started out, he would dance and leap ahead on the dusty, rock-pitted path, chasing dragonflies and birds and kicking fallen leaves until he was too tired to walk. Then he pulled at the legs of his mother's wide cotton trousers, whining, begging to be carried until she rearranged her cloth bundles and stooped down so he could climb up her back. Pretending he was riding a stallion, he wrapped his arms tight around her neck, and as she staggered forward, he dug his knees into her sides, urging her to go faster.

The memory shamed Lim, and he groaned with remorse, a terrible yearning for his mother to stoop low and carry him now.

CHAPTER FIFTEEN

Another dawn.

Less flesh, more angles and bone.

New hurts superimposed on old.

Fears that clothed like scratchy winter woolens.

Exhaustion.

Weakness.

From the size of the moon, not quite full when he began and now a crescent, Lim knew he had only been fishing eight or nine days, twelve, maybe thirteen at most. It seemed like forever.

The sharks had grown bolder. As soon as any refuse hit the water, they and other large fish surged after it. During one melee, blood from an injured fish seemed to drive the sharks mad, and he no longer dared scoop up the smaller fish that swarmed around the raft. Nor did he relieve his hands by substituting intestines for tackle. And though the stink was terrible, he saved all the fish heads, entrails, bones, and his own waste in tins and hurled them as far from the raft as possible once a day.

He wasn't eating enough to create much waste outside of urine, and as the number of fish he caught dwindled, there were fewer leavings to pitch overboard. But he could not stop entirely. Nor could he prevent the thin lines of blood that trailed from the scraps he used for bait, the jerking and flopping of his victims, and it seemed to Lim that the number of sharks he attracted was increasing.

Of the five he had counted the day before, only one was over six feet long. The others were four, perhaps four-and-a-half feet, no larger than many of the fish that swam nearby. But the sharks had large heads with small, mean eyes, an almost tangible air of menace.

Just as they swam around then under a school of fish before swooping in, their long jaws wide open, the sharks circled Lim's raft, nudged it, then dove under, coming out the other side. Sometimes they bumped so hard that their skin, rough as heavy sandpaper, shaved off barnacles and powdery flakes from the edges of the decking. What would happen if they rammed it? The raft was heavy enough that they could not capsize it and sturdy enough that it would not break. But what if they knocked him off balance and he fell into the sea? Especially at night when they were more aggressive and he was most vulnerable.

Last night he had been wakened by the unsteady tattoo of tail fins against the sides of the raft. But when he bolted upright all he saw was dark water shot with reflected starlight. His nerves screwed taut as overtight lute strings, he waited impatiently for dawn. All morning, he tried to track the ominous gray black fins and yellowish gray bodies cutting through the water. But his need to fish distracted him; the slope of the canopy cut off half the ocean from his view; and the glare, the swiftness of the sharks, and his own dullness after one more night of broken sleep made his efforts ineffectual, the strain unbearable.

He felt a tug on the line, but no weight. Had a fish robbed him of his bait? Winding the line in to check, he glimpsed a large fish clamping its jaws together. For a moment, relief that the fish was clearly not a shark overwhelmed everything else. Then he noticed the hook. Though the big fish had barely touched it, the slender twist of wire was pulled straight.

Clasping the damaged hook, the torn fragment of flesh, all that was left of the bait, to his chest, Lim sagged onto the deck, unable to control his trembling as he realized how close he had come to losing the hook, his only link to food. To life.

The fright that had gripped Lim left him weak and nauseated. If only he could get rid of the sharks he would be all right. He considered tying his knife to the end of the oar and stabbing the next shark that approached the raft. But the knife was tin, not steel, and he was more likely to anger than hurt the fish. Besides, his problem wasn't the sharks so much as the smallness of his hook.

That was it! Why hadn't he seen it before? Right now he was losing more energy than he could replace with the fish he caught. But with a larger, heavier hook, one that would support fish weighing fifteen, twenty, or even thirty pounds, a daily catch of two or three fish would take the place of his current need for forty or fifty. Not only would he save energy, but there would be less refuse and therefore less attraction for the sharks.

His mind, fragmented by an explosion of emotions, focused slowly. Metal. The hook would have to be made of metal. He scrutinized the raft. The latches on the compartments were too broad and blunt. The water tank key was too thick and heavy. The handle of the dipper? Impossible. Then perhaps the nails? Weathered and rusted, the heads studded the deck.

He would make a hook out of a nail.

Lim felt relief but no elation at the decision. Already he was puzzling over how he could safely get more hemp for the new hook. The only rope left to take apart was the lifeline that becketed the raft just above the water where sharks waited. If he stopped fishing for a few days and didn't throw out any waste at all, there would be no activity, no food to attract the sharks, and they might lose interest and swim on. But if he didn't fish, what would he eat? And if he cut the lifeline, there would be absolutely nothing left to help him get back onto the raft if he should fall again, and....

He sighed. Each time he found a solution, more problems appeared, and he was so tired. Was that why the sharks were becoming more brazen? Because they sensed his exhaustion and fear? Did they somehow know that it was only a matter of time before they would triumph?

He gazed blankly at sea and sky. How much longer before rescue came and he could give up this struggle? Or was Heaven toying with him, pretending compassion like the man in the fable?

That man had caught a turtle to make into soup. But instead of plunging it into boiling water, he placed a bamboo rod over the pot and told the turtle, "If you can walk across the pot, I will set you free."

The turtle, not wanting to die, summoned up all its will and accomplished the impossible. But when he reached the opposite side, the man said, "Please try it again."

Sheets of rain swept down from a sky suddenly darkened by clusters of black clouds that had crept near while Lim brooded. But he was too dispirited to wash down the canvas and bail. He brought the strings of drying fish under the shelter of the awning, counted thirty-seven from yesterday, thirteen from the day before. Adding the nine he had caught that morning and the two dozen or so in the food tank, he had a total of about eighty-three, two days' rations that would have to be stretched for four, maybe more, depending on when he could get to the life line. Digging out the nail would be taxing even on full rations. But if he allocated forty fish for that day, he would have only eleven for each of the next three.

Spray and rain peppered Lim's back and he crawled under the canvas bedding. If only he had someone to share his problems with, to bolster his spirits, to give him advice....

As abruptly as it had begun, the shower stopped. The sun burned a fierce yellow, and moisture steamed from the planks like steam rising from a simmering pot of thick red bean soup. Pushing aside his bedding, he reached for the water tank key, winced as his lacerated fingers wrenched open the lid.

The dipper splashed noisily and a dark wet stain snaked up the handle. At least there would be no need to ration the water. He gulped it gratefully, checked the area around the raft for sign of the sharks, saw their quick gray forms slinking through the water forty or fifty yards aft. Relieved they were no closer, he retied the strings of drying fish in the sun, then squatted in the well to choose a nail.

He rubbed his thumb over the rusted nailheads, making orange red smears that made him think of boiled sweet potatoes, revealing shiny silver tips that glittered like ash on the tips of cigarettes half smoked.... Lim shook his head. Concentrate. He must concentrate: A ship's nail was different from the nails used by carpenters ashore. Both had the sharp tips necessary for boring into wood. But the shaft of metal between the head and tip of a ship's nail was beveled, so the body was more of an elongated hexagon than a smoothly rounded cylinder.

A nail from the center of a ledge should minimize any damage. It would also allow approach from any angle and the most leverage. And if he pried one out from the deck under the curve of the awning, there would be no possibility of tripping over the hole later.

He decided to rest while the sharks were keeping their

distance and the heat was at its worst, then dig out the nail that night.

As the last rays of sunlight melted into the blue black sea, Lim untied the lower corners of the awning and pushed it onto the opposite ledge. Poking the tip of the water tank key into the wood adjacent to a nailhead in the middle of the central plank, he pushed, tentatively at first, then more insistently.

Trying to make the hole as small as possible, he dug deep rather than wide. But the light from the moon was gloomy, forcing him to work by touch as much as sight, and muscle spasms jerked his arm so that the water key flew wide of its mark, gouging broad gashes across the planks. Cursing, he tightened his grip, pitched the tip of the water tank key into the wood, and pushed.

Splinters of weathered planking peeled off sliver by sliver. Perspiration blistered the furrows creasing his forehead. A deadly numbness crept up his tensed fingers, the roots of clenched teeth.

He stopped, scooped the chips of wood into a tin, opened the water tank, dipped and drank. As the water flowed down his throat, spilling over flushed cheeks and grizzled beard, he realized he was panting, breathless as if he had dug a trench.

He leaned back on his haunches. Now that he was not working, the night air chilled, and he wrapped the canvas bedding around him while he rested, imagining steaming cups of tea, a towel wrung out of boiling hot water wiping clean his sweat and stink, a cigarette, two.

Lim's breaks and his inability to control the water tank key increased as the night wore on. But the curls of wood shavings in the tin slowly piled higher, the hole grew deeper, and by the time the moon became lost in the iridescent light of dawn, more than four inches of nail rose above a cavity the size of a baby's fist.

Where metal shaft emerged from splintered wood, Lim noticed a slight narrowing, indicating only a half inch or so of nail remained buried. If he didn't have the nail in his grasp, it might fall overboard when it finally came loose, and the thought of losing it now made him shiver. But when he tried to grab the nail and wrench it free, his sweaty, blood-flecked fingers slid up the metal shaft as if it were greased. He nudged the nail with the water key. It did not move. Should he dig further?

The sun peered over the horizon turning the sky golden, but gray dizziness blurred Lim's vision, his ability to think. He would have to rest, eat, restore some of his strength before figuring out what to do.

He slept fitfully, woke unrefreshed. In the noonday heat, the stench from yesterday's fish guts and his own waste was unbearable. Hoping to smother it, he poured the wood scraps over them, then hid the tins in the compartments below the well and studied the nail. His hands, a maze of cuts and welts, would never get the grip necessary to pull the nail out. He tried to dig. But the pressure of the water tank key against his sores hurt worse than he anticipated, and the stabs he made were feeble and uncontrolled.

He stretched out flat on his belly in front of the hole and gripped the metal spike between his teeth. Chills rippled the hairs on the back of his neck and shot down his spine, raising lumps of gooseflesh. He braced the heels of his palms against the deck and pulled. His teeth threatened to break or pull loose. Blood trickled from the roots. He spat, rotated his head.

Seizing the nailhead between his stronger back molars, he tried again, sparking a fresh wave of chills and gooseflesh. The muscles of his neck pulsed. Then throbbed. And the pain in his mouth that had begun as a twinge no sharper than when a dentist hits a nerve, grew. Spread through the roots of his teeth into his gums, his skull. Exploded.

But the nail moved.

Fractionally.

Just enough to prove it could be done.

Awash in a flood of cold sweat, Lim cut a corner out of the scrap of burlap, bunched it around the nailhead and tried again. The coarse fabric shielded him from the taste of metal, providing a cushion against the sharp, hard edges and a better grip. But nothing could ease the strain, the ache in his teeth and jaws, the taste of metal and blood.

He wrestled the nail with the teeth on one side of his jaw and then the other, his progress as imperceptible and costly as his mother's each time she plodded the eight weary li to visit her mother. Like her, he persisted.

Finally, strangling thirst compelled him to stop. Weak and uncoordinated as a marionette in the hands of a child, he spilled as much water as he drank. The water stung, then soothed his cracked, bruised lips and swollen tongue. He wanted to sleep, to sink into the soft dark womb of unconsciousness until he could emerge whole and free from pain....

Desire to live forced Lim to clamp his teeth back around the nailhead. Electric stabs jolted the base of his neck and shot through his skull each time he tensed for another pull. The roots of his teeth burned. Crescendos of pain crashed like waves, ebbing only to crest once more....

And then, suddenly, the wood released its hold, the discharge so abrupt his head jerked hard against the raft, and only locked jaws prevented the nail's loss.

CHAPTER SIXTEEN

Waiting.

Waiting for his hands to heal so he could fashion the nail into a hook.

Waiting for the sharks to move on so he could cut the rope becketing the raft to make a new fishing line.

Waiting for rescue to save him from the necessity of doing either.

Waiting.

He tried to fill the long hours by maintaining a watch, but after more than two moons of empty sea and sky, a watch was too much like a bitter parody. So he just sat. Dozed. Dreamed of cigarettes, soothing salves and plasters, and thick, fragrant congees. Tried to plan.

If he cut the lifeline from only two sides of the raft, he could retain a measure of safety yet make a strong line that was long enough so that when a fish bit, he could pay it out, allowing the hook to get well into the fish before trying to land it. And the bait must be as lively as the frogs he had used at home. Though the frogs were knocked unconscious, he had made them look like they were about to leap by inserting his hook into the animal from the hind part forward, thus concealing the metal in the frog's mouth while holding the head up. He would play a similar trick with the little fish that tumbled about, catching one with the smaller hook. Then, leaving it alive, he would pierce the tail with the larger hook so the fish could wiggle, enticing, while shielding the hook. A perfect trap.

He was impatient to try it, angry with himself for not realizing long before that he could not survive on little fish alone. Like the man who had tried to steal a bar of gold from the middle of a crowded market because the sight of the shiny gold had blinded him to the people milling around it, he seemed to snatch at the first solution his mind offered, failing to anticipate possible problems. What was he missing now?

The question nagged.

Water slapped the sides of the raft.

The planks creaked.

The stench from fish guts and his own accumulated waste grew worse.

The lacerations on his fingers and palms slowly healed.

The sharks disappeared.

Though it stretched his food ration and his patience to the limit, Lim waited another night, another day. Just to be sure. To give the scabs scarring his hands a little extra time to become new skin. Then, lying flat on his belly on the port deck, he leaned over the side as far as he dared and groped cautiously down the barnacle-crusted edge of the raft until his fingers bumped against rope.

Still nervous about sharks, he grasped the rope tenuously with his left hand, the knife with his right and began to saw. Water licked his fingers. Curious fish nuzzled close, and he jerked back, dropped the knife. Secured to a hemp tie looped around his neck, it did not fall far, and he retrieved it swiftly, tightened his grip, then hacked forcefully, anxious to finish as quickly as possible.

The knife worked so slowly it seemed to Lim it was breaking the rope strand by strand. But finally, as the sun sank close to the western horizon, he pulled sixteen feet of lifeline onto the deck.

Slick with bits of moss, rough with barnacles, and stiff from salt and sun, the lifeline resisted unraveling. As Lim separated the swatch he needed to braid the line for the new hook, a feeble breeze riffled through the strands of hemp, the rustle a bittersweet reminder of dry grasses. Land. Home.

Twisting the strands with tender fingers, he saw his mother and sister-in-law, their eyes glistening with unshed tears as they pushed their long, thick needles in and out of the layers and layers of paper and cotton wadding that made the soles for the family's shoes. A thousand stitches to every sole. A thousand twists of hemp to complete the fishing line.

And the hook still had to be made.

Using the water key as a hammer, Lim beat a curve into the nail. Each blow scraped open old sores in his hands, and pain streaked up his arms and across his back, knotting tense muscles. Sweat trickled down his cheeks, ran into his beard and mouth, tasting of tears. But he pushed on, hammering, then filing, rubbing the tip of the oddly curved nail against the water key until he wore it into a fine point.

In all, six days had passed since Lim had last fished. Without adequate food or rest, he had become weaker. Nevertheless, the prayer he murmured to Tien Hau when he cast his new line was for the hook to snare a fish that weighed at least twenty or thirty pounds.

For safety, he considered securing the new line to his wrist or the raft, then realized the twine might cut his flesh, or the fish might break the line and carry away his tackle. Winding a few extra loops around the fingers of his right hand, he let the remainder straggle loose. At the opposite end, the bait he had caught with his old tackle wriggled desperately. Unable to swim free, it could not escape below the raft like the other small fish when a large one came close and attacked, and as soon as the large fish bit, hunter would become victim. Lim chuckled. What was it his grandmother said each time a landlord snapped up more of the farmers' land? "Big fleas eat little fleas." It was the same with fish.

Knowing large fish were often close to schools of small, Lim watched for signs of breaking water. For a long time not even a ripple marred the molten surface. Then he thought he saw a quick gray shadow glide menacing. A shark? But there had been none for days! He felt a tug on his line, a sudden violent arching that shocked him into full recognition of his feeble strength. Quickly paying out the line, he dropped into the well, buttressed himself against the water tank. The metal scorched and he leaped, cursing, let loose more line as he scrambled back onto the deck where he could brace himself against a corner pole.

Afraid to let out too much line in case it tangled and just as afraid too little might make it snap, Lim played the line one way and then the other, praying the fish was not a shark, that it would tire and surrender before he did. He loosened the line, granting the illusion of freedom for a moment before winding it tighter. Silver white flashed above the surface, plunged out of sight, and muddled images bubbled as the fish resurfaced, then sank.

The line burned, cutting deep into Lim's fingers and palms. Chest heaving, he struggled for breath, control over the spasms jolting his muscles. Eventually, tense seething gave way to quiet steeled with determination, and when the fish resurfaced and he saw that, long and narrow, it was not a shark, he yanked the line taut and lunged to grasp it. A large, deeply forked tail lashed his outstretched palm, but he grabbed the part just forward of the tail, tumbling onto the deck in a tangle of thrashing fish and tackle.

The fish thumped wildly against Lim's ribs. Hugging it tight, he fumbled for his knife, plunged it awkwardly into the head behind the eyes and sawed until the severed head fell into the well, purpling the water lapping between the slats. But Lim scarcely noticed. For like the sturgeon that fights its way up the Dragon Gate rapids and is transformed into a dragon, the fish Lim had caught after all his struggles made him a dragon, a Lord who had battled death more than once — and won.

CHAPTER SEVENTEEN

The headless fish convulsed. Hanging onto the tail, Lim wedged it between his knees and ripped the knife down the spinal ridge, splitting the fish in two. There wasn't much blood, but as the masses of red and yellow organs and loops of intestines spilled out, he felt their sticky warmth, the heart still pulsing.

The skin was tough, so Lim worked from the inside out, slicing each half of the fish into steaks layer by layer. Then he cut the filets into long, one-inch thick strips. With the larger hook, he poked a hole into the top of each strip and threaded it with loops of hemp, then tied the strips to the lines between the poles.

The pile of waste on the deck outweighed the seventeen strips and Lim knew the meat would shrink further as it dried. But he refused to be disappointed. After trying to catch fifty to sixty small fish a day, two or three large ones would be easy. Or at least possible.

Landing fish that were often more than half his length was a tense business that left him breathless. Even after they were on board they continued to flail, and while Lim was weak and his hands tender, he was never sure whether he or the fish would be the victor. Once, when the scales on the fish bristled with prickly points sharp as thorns, he was unable to get a firm grip and the fish slithered off the deck. On another occasion, the fish blew up like a balloon as he pulled it out of the water. Startled, he dropped it overboard where it floated upside down for several minutes then swam away.

Most upsetting was the time he was cutting off a fish's head and he suddenly thought he saw a shark cutting through the water towards the raft. To avoid attracting sharks, he was throwing out all his refuse in the afternoon when there were no fish to be caught. Few ever surfaced to scavenge, so he was shocked when he saw the telltale fin, and he lost the fish he was holding though the head was already half off. But if a shark was part of the subsequent turmoil of boiling water clouded with blood and wild convulsing, it did not stay, and he had seen no sign of one since.

Day by day Lim's movements became more practiced and deft, and the exhaustion and mental dullness that had prevented clear thinking rolled away like a fog. He discovered the safest place to hold a fish was just behind the head or right above the tail, and a sharp blow on the head with the water tank key would knock it out, could even kill it. After he regained his strength, he sometimes broke the neck by putting a thumb in the mouth and bending the head backwards. Or he would hold the fish still by pressing down on the eyes with his thumb and middle finger, then kill it by thrusting the knife between its eyes.

Gradually, his hands healed, developed calluses. The calves of his legs hardened from the continuous balancing and bracing required when he pulled in his catch. And as the stacks of dried fish in the food tank piled higher, he felt an easing of the tension and fears that had knotted his muscles since the first torpedo exploded.

His days settled into routine. Mornings were the best

time to fish and he rose with the sun and rushed through the trivial details of living: spreading his bedding out to dry, washing, readying hooks, lines, and knife for immediate use, then folding and putting away the dried canvas in a compartment below where it would not get soiled.

He delayed eating until he had made his catch for the day, butchered it, hung the pieces on the lines to dry, and scrubbed the decks clean of blood, scales, scraps of skin, and guts. The time this took varied. Some days, the fish he caught had a sucker fish attached, giving him an unexpected bonus. But on other days, the fish might have so many fine bones that he would throw it out rather than take the risk of choking later on a bit of bone he had overlooked. Or the skin might be spotted with suspicious dark patches. Or the flesh might be too oily. Or the fish might be all head and tail with no meat to filet.

When he could not use the fish for food, Lim tried cutting up some of the meat for bait. But the fish rarely took it. Even with live bait, he found he was more likely to make a catch if he swished the bait through the water, dribbling it up and down. And when he pulled the bait rapidly across the surface of the water as though it were a flying fish skimming just before a dive, he could sometimes hook one of the large blue fish that liked to chase them.

By the time the sun reached its noonday height, he was usually ready to eat. But even if he had not caught enough to take the place of the day's rations, he would stop fishing in order to do his other chores: cleaning the knife and tackle of fish slime and rust, checking the lines, fixing any parts that had frayed or rotted, then laying them out to dry in the sun while he sharpened the edges of the knife and the point of the hook.

Though he packed pieces of the fish jerky tight together with as little air as possible between them, they had to be redried to keep them from spoiling, and he spread the old stock out on the deck regularly for sunning. Generally, he selected new strips for storage in mid-afternoon, when they were most likely to be scorched dry of any moisture from dew or spray. The least trace of damp could cause not only that piece to mildew, but the ones stacked all around it too, and if it threatened to rain, or there had just been a shower, he waited another day before taking the dried pieces down.

Despite his care, there was some spoilage. Nevertheless, the food tank now held enough fish to carry him for a week if, for any reason, he could not fish or a squall sent his victims into the deep. And with rain almost every day, he also managed to keep the water tank a little over half full.

The well-stocked tanks and his ability to fill them gave Lim a feeling of satisfaction, of mastery. And he was proud of the scrubbed decks, the lines of drying fish, and the dipper, knife, and tackle hanging neatly from the poles beneath the canvas awning, the self-sufficiency they proclaimed.

Before, he had always failed where others succeeded.

There had been no money to send his brothers to the local school, so they were sent to live in another village with an aunt whose son was a teacher. Even that only lasted a year. Yet his oldest brother had his own store in Malaya, and Gee Han had taught himself sufficient English to be an interpreter. Lim, who had gone to school for six years, still worked as a steward.

But now he had succeeded in surviving where so many before him had failed, and he was filled with new-found confidence, eager to share his victory with his parents, his betrothed. His bride.

For Gee Han's wedding feast, their father had hired six chefs from other villages to cook for twenty tables, 160 guests, and there had been steaming platters of chicken, fish, and beans, and noodles with sesame seeds.

His wedding would be larger, more sumptuous, a celebration befitting a man who had triumphed over the sea. He would spare no expense to buy the best silks for his bride's trousseau, jewelry in silver and gold, huge quantities of wine, hundreds of dragon and phoenix cakes, all of the fruits of happiness. And he would send out invitations to villages in the entire district. Feast contractors would have to build a huge outdoor stove, and the fields would be crowded with rented tables and chairs for the guests who would gasp as the coolies carrying the bride's trousseau paraded past, staggering under the weight of the lacquered gift boxes.

Finally, the red chair with the bride concealed modestly inside would arrive. Together, he and his bride would kneel and bow before the Gods of Heaven and Earth and the ancestral tablets, honor his grandmother, his father and mother, and exchange cups of wine. As they made their obeisances, he would catch glimpses of her shy smile behind the beaded veil of her headdress, a promise of her beauty. Then, in the fields, with the Old Man in the Moon beaming down at them, they would feast on delicacies while the light from hundreds of lamps and thousands of stars flickered bright as his happiness. And later, in the privacy of their marriage bed, he would conquer his bride as he had the sea.

CHAPTER EIGHTEEN

Before Lim left home, his father had told him that living in the village was like being a frog at the bottom of a well. Lim felt he had fallen back in.

Except for the coarse blue cotton cloth needed for clothing and the metal needed for tools, the villagers took almost nothing from the outside world. The rice they grew for food also provided the straw to cook it and matting to sleep on, and the oil for their lamps came from the peanuts they grew, then crushed. On the raft, with the sun to dry his fish, Lim needed no fuel to cook. Alone, he had no need for clothes. He was entirely self-sufficient.

The torrid weather reminded him of the steamy heat that allowed Hainan two crops of rice each year, and he often thought of the long stretches of irrigated fields spread out on every side of the village, the cycles of planting and harvest. First, the rice seeds, soaked in water, sown thickly in nursery beds. Next, the dry brown fields laid under water and ploughed by water buffalo, with the driver, his father, wading up to his knees. Then, standing ankle deep in mud and water, his father drilling holes in orderly rows, his sister-in-law dropping little clumps of green seedlings into each hole, his mother tamping earth about the roots. And when the rice plants bore ears full and round, his father cutting the stalks by hand, bundling them for Lim's mother and sister-in-law to beat into a sieve placed over a wooden tub. Bit by bit they winnowed the grain by tossing it into the air for the wind to blow out the chaff, then spread the golden grains out thinly in the sunshine, regularly turning them with a rake-like tool until they became dry enough to store without rotting.

Remembering, Lim imagined the sea around him as fields. On the horizon, the water shimmered silver like paddies just laid under water. Closer to the raft, the jade green water was pure as fields carpeted with green shoots that became the warm gold of harvest wherever sunbeams danced. Only his fields yielded a daily harvest of fish.

He was as dependent as any farmer on the whims of Heaven, and like them, he studied the sky and the sea, his earth. He could smell a wind before it came, and he knew that thin-veiled clouds and a wind that veered abruptly from northeast to northwest meant a storm. As soon as the ocean grew darker, becoming a drab olive or steel gray, he secured his tackle, took down the fish, and readied the canvas for bailing. But there were still surprises.

One moment the sky could be a perfect fish belly silver and the sea a glaring polished mirror, and the next he could be tossing in a raging mass of short, hard waves, his skin slick from foam splintering into high, thin spray. Sometimes the wind howled through the rigging, filling the canvas awning like a sail, sending the raft skimming above moving walls of water. Crouched low, Lim held his breath and braced himself as the tops of waves washed over him. The sense of movement was exhilarating. At the same time, it made him feel uneasy, as though he were on the edge of an abyss, and he was always relieved when the wind died and the canvas stopped flapping.

Twice he caught a drab, colorless fish that reacted explosively by leaping out of the water repeatedly, trying to shake out the hook. Though nervous he might lose his tackle, Lim battled them until they became exhausted, just as he had the shark.

He did not realize it was a shark at first. The day before he had sighted a pair of fins that he was sure were sharks, but when they soared into the air and spread, he saw they were a ray's fins. And before that, he had mistaken a dolphin for a shark until it broke the surface blowing and squeaking. So even though the fish thrashing at the end of the line looked like a shark, he ignored the signs, telling himself he was mistaken.

Only after he landed it did he see that the fish was indeed a shark. It was small, under three feet. But killing it added to his confidence, and he felt as if he had completed the final initiation into the watery world ruled by Dragon Lords.

Living on the raft required more effort than living in the village where his parents had provided food and shelter. On the other hand, there were none of the often tiresome concerns and complications that come from people, none of the obligations, and as the third moon neared its fullness, Lim felt a weightlessness, a sense of contentment, even joy.

While he worked, he sang songs from his childhood, snatches of famous tunes from operas that were full of beauty and emotion. He cut up smaller fish with extra care, strung the vertebrae onto the end of a line, and threw them into the water where fish picked them clean. Then he decorated the raft with the skeletons, attaching them to the lines overhead with twists of tin that winked in the sun.

In the late afternoon, when his work was done, he often lay on the deck and watched the skeletons and bits of tin dance in the breeze. Or he gazed up at the clouds, staring at their changing shapes until they became mythical creatures. A silken lion perhaps, with bulging eyes, shaggy ears, and a big bushy tail, jumping, running, rolling on its back, scratching at a flea, or playing with a ball. Or a dragon, many dragons, swirling in a night sky. But when the Queen of Heaven commanded them to draw in their tails, a sudden gust of wind would sweep clean the floor of Heaven, exposing the stars that made up the Heavenly River, the Cowherd and the Weaver Maid on opposite banks.

The Weaver Maid, the seventh daughter of the Sun God, had always lived in Heaven where she wove the fabrics used for making the immortals' clothing. But the Cowherd had once been an ordinary villager like Lim. Then his cow, who was magical, told him how he too could gain immortality. "The Weaver Maid often comes down from Heaven to bathe in the nearby stream. The next time she comes, hide her clothes and refuse to return them until she consents to be your bride."

When the Cowherd followed his cow's instructions, the Weaver Maid agreed to marry him, and they lived happily together for three years. Then the Gods and Goddesses ran out of silks and brocades to make new clothing, so they forced the Weaver Maid to return to her old job.

The Cowherd was heartbroken, and the cow, pitying his master, said, "Kill me and use my skin as a magic carpet to fly up and rejoin your wife."

Again, the Cowherd did as his cow instructed. But just as he was about to reach his wife, the Weaver Maid's mother, in a fit of jealousy, drew a line on the floor of Heaven with her hairpin and created the Heavenly River to separate them forever.

Within sight of each other, the two remain apart. Except for one night each year when all the magpies in the world come together and form a bridge across the

Heavenly River with their wings so the Weaver Maid can cross and join her husband.

Looking up at the clusters of small stars glowing like the fireflies that dotted the fields back home, Lim thought of his betrothed and himself, separated by the sea. His happiness became tinged with loneliness, and he imagined all the flying fish in the world coming together and forming a bridge so his betrothed could come to him. Only he would never let her leave.

Close to full, the moon shone so bright that Lim, lying on his belly, felt he was floating on a fantastical Heavenly Lake. From the side hidden by the canvas awning, the dark silhouette of a flying fish appeared, soaring higher and more gracefully than any Lim had seen before. Half asleep, he wondered idly whether it might be a bird. A magpie, he mused, the first of all the magpies in the world coming to form a bridge between him and his betrothed.

A call, liquid and aching, and the hard beating of wings broke his reverie. This was a real bird, not a dream. Afraid any movement would frighten it, he froze as the bird flew closer, stopped about ten feet short of the raft in a sort of hover, then plunged head first into the sea. With its long tail and wings trailed back, it looked like a falling lance, and when it vanished, Lim felt a strange, unexpected pain.

Cautiously he eased himself forward, heard a sudden flapping of wings, another hard, sharp cry. Pulling himself up onto his knees, he grabbed a corner pole to steady himself and peered around the blind created by the awning. The bird was circling directly above, its pointed white wings and long, narrow tail feathers almost translucent in the moonlight.

Still caught between dream and wakefulness, Lim wondered if the bird might be sheung yeung, the fabulous bird that could dry up whole sections of the sea. But the water around the raft shimmered undiminished, and when the bird lighted on top of the pole Lim held, he saw it had two tiny feet where sheung yeung had only one.

For a moment, the bird teetered on its perch as though undecided whether to stay or go. Then, crying shrilly, it took off, its wing-beat steady and determined. The high-pitched trill and long, pointed wings made Lim think of a gull. But the rapid direct flight with only short periods of glides, graceful flaps, and long soars differed from what he remembered of a gull's more leisurely flight. And it was smaller, the size of a pigeon. Or was it the rapidly widening distance between the raft and bird that made it seem small?

All too soon the ghostly gleam of white feathers blurred, became part of the night sky. But the splatter of green droppings on the edge of the deck beneath the pole proved the bird's reality, and Lim felt a rush of excitement, for a bird meant trees and earth and mountains and rock. Land.

CHAPTER NINETEEN

As a steward, Lim had often felt impatient for land, a break from the boredom of a daily schedule that never varied and the grind of continuous service. During the long days and nights before docking, he tossed in his bunk, puffing on one cigarette after another, counting the hours until he would have solid ground under his feet once more. If his duties allowed, he ran up onto the deck as soon as landfall was sighted and watched eagerly while the ship steamed into the harbor. Then, once ashore, he rubbed the heels of his shoes against the tar or dirt of the road and walked the town, looking at the colorful displays in the stores and stalls, eating fresh food, going to a movie or a woman.

There was a sameness to his days now, but the ever-present element of surprise prevented monotony, and he liked the rhythm that came from his daily rituals. With Heaven smiling on him, giving him plenty of fish and rain but no bad storms, the fears that had almost paralyzed him at first had dissipated, and he felt no more compelled to leave the raft than he had the village.

He remembered how his father's sun-blackened back blended with the soil when he stooped over a field, how the furrows of his hands were ingrained with dirt no matter how hard he scrubbed them. Just so, salt crusted every crevice of Lim's body, and he felt as much a part of the sea as a farmer does of the land. Nevertheless, the day after he saw the bird, he could not quell the same sense of anticipation he had felt as a child before a holiday, and while he fished, gutted, and hung up his catch, he squinted expectantly across the water and the sky above.

As the morning slid past with no sign of birds or a landfall, Lim thought of the way flocks of gulls used to swoop after the refuse the cook's helpers threw overboard. He could not recall whether the birds appeared whenever scraps were dumped or only when the ship was near land. But it suddenly occurred to him that the bird he had seen might have come from a ship's rail rather than land. The thought brought back the memory of the ship that had turned away, and bitterness surged, sticking in his throat like bile, spoiling his pleasure in the day.

Dusk gathered, became night. But Lim, churning from the memories and emotions the bird had stirred, was too restless to sleep, and he squatted on the ledge, gnawing his lips, twisting his fingers through his tangle of beard and hair.

Eating his evening meal, he had tried to figure out if it was the bird, the prospect of land, the memory of the ship that had turned away, or something else entirely that had unsettled him. But the effort only frustrated him further.

Once, as a child, he had tried to gather mimosa. The green fronds were so delicate and pretty he wanted to take some home, but each time he plucked a branch, the fronds closed up tight and ugly. He tried snatching them, then sneaking up slowly. But no matter what he did, they clamped shut at his touch, reopening only after he backed off. Eventually, he had given up and let them be. Now he tried to do the same with his thoughts, abandoning what he could not understand in the hope of reclaiming the peace that had been his before the bird came.

He spread out his bedding, slid between the canvas and called up his favorite fantasies. His triumphant return home to his betrothed. The banquet followed by the wedding night. A chain of smokes....

Thoughts fleeting as darting fish distracted him. He rolled over on his side and propped himself up on an elbow. In the bright light of the rising moon, the stars slowly receded. The arm he was leaning on fell asleep.

Getting up to massage it, he noticed a flash of white a few yards aft. Except for the long tail feathers that swirled like streamers in the gentle breeze, the bird could have been a bleached out, long-winged pigeon or a dove, its white feathers barely distinguishable from the silver of the sea. Watching it fly low over the water, splashing onto the surface like a seaplane, or bobbing in the water with its neck held high and tail angled jauntily upward, Lim realized the bird might not need land or a ship's rail, and he wondered how long it had been close by, whether it was the bird from the night before that had been floating nearby, or a different one that had just come.

The bird glided, then wheeled, using the long plume on its tail like a rudder so that it could turn sharp angles while its wings remained more or less still. Like a cyclist who uses his momentum at the end of a freewheel downhill to take him up part of the next slope, it rose with a gust of wind, then dove with an unhurried opening of wings. A simple tilt of its wings upward increased its lift while a lilt up with vigorous flapping caused it to stall, and it seemed capable of flying forever without tiring. But finally, like an acrobat who has completed a performance, it banked, wobbled its wings, and cried out in a high-pitched trill, then vanished into the night, leaving Lim feeling strangely soothed.

A shower fell late the next day. He knew from the thinness of the clouds and the intensity of the sun that it would be brief and the water tank was more than half full, so he chose to scrub himself clean rather than bail. The rain lasted just long enough for him to get rid of the worst of the salt, and he settled down to his evening meal with a buoyant sense of well-being, an expectation he hardly dared admit. He was not disappointed.

The bird returned with the moon that night and when other birds followed, Lim began to feel like the owner of a duck boat. While fishing in the river at home, he had seen boatloads of ducks go by, the master eyeing the river banks, looking for suitable pasture for his flock as he plied his oar. When there was sufficient food, he pulled ashore and the ducks marched down the gangplank to feed for a day or two before their master called them back and moved on.

Lim's flock was not as obedient as the ducks, but in three nights, it grew from one to six, and the bird from the first night was always among them. He recognized it by its pure white color and long tail feathers. The others were dark with white underparts and short, rounded tails, and they flew differently, with alternate short bursts of flapping and long glides, banking low over the surface on stiff wings.

Though their bodies seemed heavier, these birds were also skillful aerial acrobats, thrusting themselves straight into the air, then shooting down into the water without seeming to move their long, narrow wings. But they never came close to the raft. The white bird did. Like a fidgety child, it did not stay in one place long, hopping from a corner pole to the lines holding the fish, pecking at the meat, then swooping down into the sea, returning briefly to the water tank, flying up onto the top of another pole, abruptly switching to yet another. But Lim enjoyed its antics, and though the birds always disappeared into a secret existence of their own before dawn, their presence during the night added a new dimension, new pleasure to his life on the raft.

In the space of the few nights it took for the moon to fill out completely, the birds became as much a part of the rhythm of Lim's nights as fishing was of his days, and he was totally unprepared when they vanished with the moon. They might have been out there still. Once or twice it seemed he did hear the hard beating of the larger birds' wings, a gentle sigh that might have been birds flying overhead. But the sliver of new moon did not shed enough light for him to see beyond the glimmer of white awning, and he felt deserted, even betrayed.

Reasoning that if the birds had come from either land or a ship, he would have seen signs of one or the other by now, he pushed both possibilities out of his mind. But he continued looking for the birds. The second night of the new moon, he felt a faint stir of air that came from whirring wings, heard a dull slapping as strips of dried meat, fish skeletons and twists of metal collided, caught a flash of white flitting near.

Excited, he leaped up without thinking, knocking over an empty tin. A screech of alarm rose above the clatter and the bit of white disappeared into the deeper darkness Lim's eyes could not penetrate. But its cry and the snow white feather floating down told him that the white bird with the long tail feathers had returned.

He did not see the darker birds then or on subsequent nights. But under the cover of darkness, the white bird became increasingly brave. From teetering nervously on a line or the top of a pole, it began to roost as calmly as a chicken in a hen house. Now and then, it perched on the edge of the deck near Lim's feet, and if he remained absolutely motionless, it sometimes hopped across the canvas bedding covering his legs. Once, when he was sitting up, his back against a corner pole, it landed on his shoulders, then dropped down onto his lap before taking off again, its air impertinent, almost teasing, as though it were daring Lim to try to catch it.

That night, Lim dreamed of One Eye, his chick, only she was white like the bird and they were on the raft together. During the bright hours of sunlight, she hopped around the deck or hovered overhead, playfully nipping his fingers while he hung strips of fish up to dry, preening while he washed. Nestled in the crook of Lim's arm, they shared the canvas bedding, her warm pulse beat throbbing against his own as they slept, and there was a newly laid egg beneath her when they rose at dawn. Piercing the shell with the point of the hook, Lim sucked, savoring the taste, the thick richness of yolk and albumen sliding down his throat.

After the first week out of port, when all the fresh food on board was eaten, the meals on the *Benlomond* had been drearily repetitious, which was another reason why Lim looked forward to reaching land. At home there had also been little variety to the meals of boiled taro and sweet potato and congee. But there were festivals with special treats that he could look forward to. And in between there might be salty pickled turnips, a smear of shrimp paste, or a sticky piece of peanut brittle. But for almost two moons now he had eaten nothing except fish.

A few times, the monotony of his diet had spurred him to cautious experimentation. Once, when he discovered a smaller fish inside a large fish's stomach, he ate it without drying it first. Partially digested, it had tasted cooked, almost delicious. On another occasion he caught a greenish fish with protruding teeth that made it look like a parrot. Cutting it up, drying, then eating it, he had pretended the fish was a pigeon. But hours later, his mouth and lips and throat began to tingle. Then he felt weak and chilled, and afraid the fish might have been poisonous, he rammed his first and second fingers down his throat, forcing himself to vomit until his stomach was completely empty.

Though he had found little fish in the stomachs of fish he had caught since then, he had not dared to eat them. And he threw back any fish with protruding teeth or spiny backs, bellies that ballooned when touched, anything that might be at all suspicious. Not daring to experiment, he was limited to dried fish and tasteless water, and eating was becoming the most difficult chore of each day.

If he caught the bird, however, he would have eggs to break the monotony of his diet. Maybe. The bird could be like One Eye. Or a male. Or perhaps this kind of bird only laid eggs during a certain season, or only on land. But it was worth a try.

CHAPTER TWENTY

One of the teachers at Wah Nam, the mechanics school in Hong Kong, liked to feed cicadas to the birds he raised, and to win his approval, the students caught the insects as gifts for him. Over a period of time, the students discovered that the insects burrowed into the earth to lay their eggs. Then, when the eggs became ugly, wingless pupa, they crawled out of the ground and climbed up the nearest tree trunk under cover of darkness. Some time during the night they shed their skin and released their wings, and the males, trying to attract mates, began to sing. The noise also attracted the students. They came with small tins tied to the ends of long bamboo poles, and at the bottom of each tin was a dollop of starchy paste. When the tins were thrust up into the branches of the noisiest trees, the cicadas that crawled in were unable to escape because the sticky paste made their wings useless.

Now Lim tried to figure out how he could catch the bird. It was too large to be trapped in a tin. That left his hands or some kind of snare made of string. There was still some hemp left from the lifeline he had cut, and he braided two strings with loops that could be tightened around the bird's legs, holding it captive without hurting it.

As dusk gathered, he laid the strings on the deck within easy reach and waited for his chance. The bird, landing on the edge of the deck, often ran forward, rather like a child who is unable to stop his momentum after running down a hill. He might be able to grab it then, but it would probably be safer to wait until its wings were folded tight. Another opportunity might come while it was preening. Twisting its head on its long, supple neck until it could rub its beak just above its tail, it delved in and out of its ruffled feathers, smoothing and cleaning with its beak, its concentration intense.

Rushing to finish the snares before dark, Lim had not eaten his evening meal. He wasn't hungry now, but he was too jittery to sit still entirely, so he gnawed a piece of fish jerky. Before he could finish it, he saw white feathers flitting mothlike over the black water. His mouth salivating in anticipation of the eggs he hoped the bird would provide, he dropped the jerky onto his lap and cautiously felt the deck beside him until he found the strings.

The bird landed on the deck near Lim's outstretched legs, sprinkling him with a shower of salty drops that dripped down the soles of his feet, tickling. The desire to scratch made him shiver, and he curled his fingers into fists in an effort to control the urge. A muscle in his calf twitched, and the piece of half-eaten jerky slid off his lap onto the deck. Scolding, the bird flew onto the lines of fish overhead.

Its abrupt flight startled Lim. He had thought the bird too familiar with him and the raft to frighten so easily. But he was glad of the warning: If he failed in his first attempt to catch it, the bird was not likely to give him a second chance.

An unsteady rat-tat-tat came from above. Straining, he could just make out the bird pecking one of the fish skeletons just like the schoolmaster's birds pecked at the bones attached to the bars of their cages. Moving no more than an inch at a time, he tucked his outstretched legs under him in a cross between a squat and a crouch. Then he transferred the braided hemp snares into his left fist, leaving the right hand free to grab the bird.

It swooped down onto the food tank, then hopped into the well. Using its long tail like an elevator, it jumped up to the opposite deck. Was he imagining it, or was the bird agitated? Was it possible that it sensed Lim's ferment, the excitement coursing through him? Did it somehow realize it was in danger?

Tension tightened Lim's muscles and he could feel the beginnings of a cramp in his right foot. But he dared not move. The bird hopped onto the ledge where Lim crouched, discovered the bit of fish Lim had dropped earlier. It began to peck, its back at an angle to him. Impaling the bird with his eyes, he slid his right hand slowly across the eighteen inches of deck separating them and grabbed.

He had one leg. Two. Wings flapped furiously. Clamping them down with his other hand, he dropped the strings. His legs, numb from crouching so long, buckled. As he fell, he thrust his arms forward to prevent crushing the bird, rolled onto his side. The bird's head hurtled back and forth, wildly pecking at Lim's fingers, the air, the deck, itself, and cries of rage and fear ripped the night. Feathers flew, and Lim jerked a hand loose to search for the strings he had dropped. Legs kicked. Wings beat desperately. Seizing both legs and wings, he squeezed his victim mercilessly and dropped, cursing, into the well of the raft, kneeling so he would be at eye level with the deck, the strings. Down and droppings littered the planks like sullied snowflakes, and he leaned close, struggling to hold the bird still. Beak stabbed fingers. Claws scratched palms. The snare of clenched hands became slick with droppings, blood.

Finally he saw one string. Whipping out a hand, he snatched it, twisted it round thrashing wings, feet, and head. Trussed and helpless, the bird screeched its anger still, and for a long time the deck pounded with its body's hopeless thumping. Eventually, it quieted, and the only sounds were Lim's raspy, ragged breaths and the slap of water against the raft.

He leaned over the edge of the deck, splashed water over his face, arms, and chest. The salt water stung his wounds and he wondered why he had fought so hard for the bird. Was the possibility of an egg, a break in his monotonous diet, really that important to him? Or, once begun, had he continued the struggle to capture the bird simply to prove he could?

He reached over to pick up the bird. Beak snapping, it lurched, screeching, from Lim's touch. He pulled back undaunted. He had seen the teacher at Wah Nam tame birds as wild as this one, first teaching them to eat from their master's hand, then sliding a wire collar with a short chain around each of their necks.

The teacher had taught the birds to catch seed thrown into the air and to fetch little paper flags. And there was a neighbor in the tenement across from the school who raised pigeons on the roof and trained them to come home to roost each night though they flew free during the day. There was no reason why he couldn't tame this bird just as they had tamed theirs. The only question was whether it would then lay eggs.

Fumbling around in the gloomy light of the new moon, he made two new cords to leash the bird. But untying it was impossible. Until he remembered a trick his mother had taught him. Holding the trussed bird down on the deck with one hand, he used a finger to trace ever-widening circles in the bird's line of vision until it became hypnotized. While the bird was in a trance, he untied it, noosed one string around each leg and then looped both around a corner pole under the low side of the canvas awning.

Once out of the trance, the bird flexed its wings as it would before flight, but no sooner had it taken wing than the twine jerked it short, and it plummeted back onto the deck, dazed and confused. After several more thwarted attempts, it shrieked angrily, pecking at the twine that bound it. Its wings beat furiously, then frantically. The string tangled, and the nooses tightened, rubbing its legs raw. Lim filled a tin with water and another with dried fish, then pushed them within the bird's reach. But the bird upset both tins, knocking one overboard with its wild kicking.

It took all night for the bird to wear out its strength. When Lim offered it fish at dawn, it did not struggle or cry or kick the tin aside. Neither did it eat. Nevertheless, Lim felt encouraged, and he crooned to it softly, all the time edging across the well until he was almost at its side. But when he reached out to scratch its head in the spot One Eye had particularly enjoyed, the bird backed away, crying its fear.

Seeing the bird for the first time in the bright light of day, he realized there was a pinkish tinge to the white feathers, that it had a greenish-yellow bill, blue black facial skin, and dark gray feet. And when it continued to refuse food that day and the next, Lim began to wonder if the bird did not need to eat because it was the five-colored sparrow, the one the Gods used as a messenger.

The possibility made him nervous, for no good ever came to those who tried to trick immortals. But perhaps the bird was a gift, a reward from the Gods for his triumph over the sea? No. It belonged to this world, not the Gods'. Hadn't he seen it dive for fish while there was a full moon? And the droppings he had scrubbed off the deck the morning before were real enough. With time, he would win the bird's trust. Then it would eat. He just had to be patient.

By the afternoon of the third day, the bird accepted Lim's caresses and it drank water out of a tin Lim held. But there was no joy in his victory. Since it had given up struggling, the bird had barely moved. Quiet as a brood hen, but with none of its pride or purpose, it continued to refuse fish, dried or raw, the bits Lim chewed for it, the live ones he caught to tempt it with. Without nourishment or preening, the sleekly glossy feathers were turning dull, lifeless as the black beads of eyes empty of will.

Scratching the bird's head, Lim thought of the dragonflies and butterflies he had trapped as a child. Though he kept them in willow baskets filled with grasses and flowers, they had rarely lived more than a day or two.

"You're as foolish as the Marquis of Lu," his father had scolded when he found Lim chasing pale green dragonflies until they flew, confused, into his cages.

"When a seagull flew into his city," his father continued, "the Marquis welcomed it in the temple and ordered the best music and grandest sacrifices for it. But the bird remained in a daze, not swallowing a single morsel of food or drinking a single cup of wine.

"After three days, the bird died because the Marquis was entertaining the seagull the way the Marquis liked to be entertained, never once considering what the seagull wanted."

Neither the story nor repeated failures had stopped Lim from trapping the insects, and once he did catch a dragonfly that lived almost a week before it died. But the teacher at Wah Nam had birds he claimed were five years old and more. Why was he so successful? Did it have something to do with the walks the students took the birds on each morning?

"Move your arms as though they were tree branches in a brisk wind and swing the cages while you walk," their teacher had instructed. "That way the birds must flex their muscles to keep their balance and they will get the exercise they need for good singing."

Now Lim wondered if the walks also gave the birds an illusion of freedom, if a similar trick might work with this bird. He could not make a cage for it or take it for walks, but he could clip its wings so it could not fly more than a few feet, then cut the cords binding it to the raft.

Hacking at the feathers with the pemmican tin knife would be rough, but he could hypnotize the bird. Then, when it woke without the twine chafing its legs, it would think itself free. Of course, its inability to really fly would be frustrating at first, but it would get used to it soon enough. Hadn't he?

Perhaps. But only because he wanted to live. The bird did not. If he did not let it go, it would almost certainly die. And its death would be on Lim's hands.

Slowly, regretfully, he loosened the nooses around the bird's legs, setting it free. It was too weak to do little more than stumble and too mistrustful to eat, even after Lim backed into the farthest corner of the raft. But when night came and Lim retreated under his canvas bedding, he could hear pecking, sharp and steady, the splash of water, the muffled sounds of preening.

In the morning, he saw the bird resting on the water a little way off. Not wanting to frighten it with any kind of disturbance, he did not fish, and when morning stretched into afternoon and the bird remained, he felt a gladness, a spurt of hope the bird might choose to stay. But just before night came again, it took off. Though its flight seemed weak and listless, the bird shrank smaller with each throb of its wings, swiftly becoming a pale ghost on the gray horizon, then a memory.

CHAPTER TWENTY-ONE

A broom star, a warning from Heaven of calamity, fell that night. Unable to sleep, Lim tossed restlessly, tried to convince himself that what he had seen was not a comet but a bird, his bird, plunging into the ink-black sea for fish. But the sound of the measure scraping across the bottom of the water tank when he dipped for water in the morning and the pungent, unmistakable odor of mildew that greeted him when he opened the food tank told him otherwise.

While holding the bird captive, he had concentrated all his efforts on trying to soothe it, neglecting his chores. There had been two squalls but, thinking the water tank well filled, he decided not to disturb the bird by bailing. Instead, he drank water straight out of the canvas catchment. Fishing only to tempt the bird, he did not bother to dry what he caught, simply pulling down strips of meat from the lines to eat whenever he was hungry. Now the lines were bare, and because he had not aired the stacks of jerky in the food tank, they were spoiled. Seething with self reproach, he sorted through the mess, redrying the few pieces that were salvageable, casting his lines to catch more.

His luck, however, seemed to have flown with the bird. Though he spent more time fishing, he did not catch as many fish as before. Nor were those he caught as large. The heat and humidity, always oppressive, became smothering, the moisture so heavy it rotted the meat before it could dry. Yet there was almost no rain. Each time he saw rain clouds moving his way, Lim quickly readied the canvas awning, rinsing off the worst of the salt with seawater. But the clouds rarely came close. Or it poured on either side of the raft while the sky directly above remained blue.

Before becoming skilled at cutting up fish, Lim's hand had often slipped, and whenever his knife had hit a backbone, he had noticed fluid leaking out. Now, hoping to stretch his water supply, he split open individual vertebrae deliberately with his knife and teeth and sucked out the spinal fluid. He also found he could activate saliva if he continued to chew the bone even after all the liquid was gone. And he made and drank fish juice.

At first he diced scraps of raw fish, wrapped the bits in the piece of burlap, and twisted the fabric to squeeze out the juice which he collected in a tin. The taste was surprisingly pleasant, rather like clams. But the process of cutting and squeezing the fish was tedious, consuming energy he could barely muster. Still, memory of his earlier attempt to eat raw fish made Lim hesitant to try a more direct method for getting the fish juice. Then the last bit of burlap rotted, forcing him to give in. Pretending the raw fish was sugarcane, he gnawed the lump until it was dry. Not wanting to waste, he swallowed the lumpy residue of desiccated meat as well.

Shortly afterwards, his belly started cramping before bowel movements, and he worried that he might be getting worms from eating raw meat. But when he checked his feces, he found none. He also noticed that eating the fish raw made him less thirsty than eating it dried, that some fish held more fluid in their flesh than others, that there were differences in the taste of the meat. Desperate to add variety and liquid to his diet, he tried eating the organs.

The kidneys, an irregular mass under the backbone, were quite good, and the liver and heart, separated only by a membrane, were both tasty. There was another red glandular mass that he sometimes ate though he could not identify it. And one night, when a school of smelt swarmed under the raft so thickly that he was able to scoop them up by the handfuls, he ate them whole. But there were parts he still would not try: gristly looking tongues, stomachs with their jet black or pale linings and tubular sacs, intestines.

Eating most of the fish now, he was wasting less. Yet he could not seem to rebuild the reserves he had lost, and the empty tanks coupled with the Gods' warning of disaster nagged at him. The daily grind and the pressure of having only himself to provide for all his needs gradually drained away the pleasure he had taken in his self-sufficiency. He became irritated over minor inconveniences such as a frayed line that had to be repaired, absurdly depressed if he so much as stumbled or lost a bit of bait.

When he attempted to rebuild his reserves by cutting his rations, he was unable to sustain the energy he needed to push himself through the myriad of chores that crowded each day. Even on full rations, he was losing weight, and at night, the canvas bedding no longer provided adequate padding between his fleshless limbs and the hard planking of the deck.

Lying wide-eyed, he tried to deny the void the birds' absence had carved, the burgeoning loneliness that throbbed like a dull but omnipresent toothache. Hadn't he always been a loner who walked by himself?

In the village, there had always been a frog hunt, basketball or shuttlecock game he could join, someone to race or wrestle, a storyteller to listen to. Yet he was more likely to climb a hill to fly a kite alone or hide among reeds and bushes to fish in solitude. It was the same on board the ships he served. There had been card games, heated discussions over working conditions and the war, nostalgic talk of home, excited plans for women at the next port. But seeking privacy, he spent most of his off-duty hours alone, leaning against the taffrail, smoking, staring at the wake.

Of course, at home, no matter where he went, he could still see sun-bronzed farmers working in the fields; smell the smoke curling up from cooking fires; hear the chatter of women, the slap of wet clothes beaten against rocks, the sing-song chant of students reciting lessons, the excited shuffling and cheering of boys crowded round a cricket fight. All the sights and smells and sounds that made him a part of a warm, safe, unbreakable whole. And on board, he was never beyond the sound of the crew's voices, their laughter, the smell of their cigarettes, the strong, unspoken bonds of family and community that made him one of them whether he wanted it or not.

Lim sighed. How could the solitude he had snatched then be compared to the isolation forced upon him now? Those hours alone had been few and therefore precious. But more than three moons had passed with no human voice, no touch except his own.

Yet he had been content before the birds came. Bitterly, he regretted the peace they had shattered, and he imagined the bird he had set free, plucked, pulled, salted, and flattened by a smashing blow on the breast bone with the flat of a kitchen cleaver, hanging in the sun, drying and shrinking into a waxy, salty, highly flavored treat. Or roasted until its skin crackled honey brown and crisp; its feet steamed separately in garlic, black bean, and red pepper sauce, chewy and crunchy. Or perhaps, as though it were a little rice bird, he would eat it skin, bones, and all.

The appetizing fragrance of Lim's imaginings caused a rush of saliva. Juices churned, twisting his pinched belly. He shifted uncomfortably, thought he saw a flock of birds aft. But when he scooted down to the edge of the deck and looked more carefully, he saw they were a school of flying fish. He slumped back down into the bedding, angry at himself for making such a stupid mistake. For the flight of the flying fish was mere imitation, and they did not belong in the birds' sky any more than he belonged in the fish's watery world.

Too tense to lie still, he fidgeted, smoothing the bedding, tugging at his wisps of beard, the tangles in his hair, wishing he could unsnarl his thoughts as easily. Eventually, however, exhaustion forced sleep. Yet even this, his only release, was tainted by mockeries of childhood imaginings.

In his dreams then, he had been the legendary Monkey King, with special magic that conquered demons and allowed escape from cremation in a fiery crucible or imprisonment in a mountain. He had only to expel his breath to be propelled into the air where magic winds sent him and his loyal companions soaring up the Heavenly River. Using clouds as trapezes, they cavorted between stars, tossing silver raindrops with a flick of their tails, batting diamond snowflakes and golden hailstones with feet and wings until all of Heaven became a colorful dazzle of joyous activity.

But in his dreams now there was no special magic, no loyal companions. He was alone, trapped on the golden sea of Buddha's palm. And though he leaped ten thousand leagues and more, he could not escape Buddha's grasp.

Kneeling in the well, Lim rubbed the blade of his knife against the sides of the ledges to clean it. The air was so moist, it seemed to him he could actually see the rust growing back as quickly as he scraped it off. Sweat trickled down his forehead, blurring his vision. He smeared his face dry with the back of his hand. But more sweat dripped down from his thick thatch of hair.

He leaned back against his haunches. Water licked his feet and ankles, cooling. But his throat felt so parched he could hardly swallow. He took a vertebra from the tin where he kept some, bit down hard. He had already sucked this one more than once, but gnawing it and pretending it was the pit of a sour plum helped.

He had promised himself he would wait until dusk before he took a proper drink. Would he make it? Squinting up at the sky, he thought he saw wings glittering dark silver. He blinked impatiently. Was he never going to stop seeing birds that were not there!

He opened his eyes. As he had expected, the wings were gone. No. They were still there, a little farther to the west and higher than before. And they belonged to neither fish nor bird, but a plane!

As though from a great distance, he saw himself leaping to his feet, waving, shouting. He spluttered, almost choked, spat out the bone. "Help!" he cried. "I've been here for months! Help!"

Jumping, squeezing his eyes into tiny slits against the glare, he lost sight of the plane. But the faint hum of engines and the vapor trail it was scratching across the polished bowl of sky were clear. Fired with absurd hope, he continued to shout until his voice and the slap of waves against the raft were the only sounds once more. Even then, he skittered around the raft like an ant on a hot pan, wondering if the pilot would return, if another plane would come.

His head throbbed. What if the plane came at night? Could he use the torch? Shine it on the canvas? Reaching up the corner pole to where his fishing lines were coiled and tied, Lim grasped the fish hook made from the spring of his torch, saw what he already knew: The twist of wire would never work again as a spring.

He heard the steady beat of engines. Another plane. And from the sound of it, this one was much closer. What could he do to attract the pilot's attention? Waving and shouting were stupid. A waste of time and strength. With the awning covering the raft and the roar of engines wiping out his cries, how would the pilot ever notice him?

To be seen, he must make himself distinct from the sea. But he had lost the orange life jacket, the only bit of color, overboard; he had wasted all his flares on the ship that refused to rescue him. The grubby white square of canvas awning blended right into the shimmering white gold sea. If he lowered the awning, the sun-bleached planks of the raft would be just as impossible for a pilot to see. And his own skin, darkened to mahogany and streaked with dried salt, made him a mere splinter of the raft.

Perhaps if he shook the dropped awning? No, it was too awkward and heavy, would look too much like a rippling in the ocean. But a flag... To a pilot, it would be so small, like a tiny pin stuck in a lapel on Flag Day. But if he waved it frantically enough, the staccato, darting movements might attract the pilot's attention.

Snatching his knife, Lim hacked a piece of canvas from the strip he used for bedding. Then he stabbed holes down one side of the jagged square and tied the cloth to the wide end of an oar with bits of string. Worried the plane would be gone by the time the flag was finished, his eyes scoured the sky while he worked. He could find no telltale trail of vapor, but the beat of engines pulsed steadily, and he plunged on.

Suddenly he realized that what he thought was the throb of engines was actually a pounding in his head. Disgusted, he hurled the flagged oar into the well. Then, as abruptly as he had thrown it, he swooped the flag back up onto the deck. The plane might return. Or there could be another plane. But a plane would come. It had to. And when it did, he would be ready.

CHAPTER TWENTY-TWO

Usually the air turned chill as soon as the sun dipped below the horizon. But today, after the glare diffused into dusk then night, the heat remained, thick as a winter quilt. Lim spread his bedding and stretched out on top of it. Because he used no cover, there were more layers of padding between him and the deck. But the canvas scratched; the air, cloyingly humid, made breathing a chore; and he could not settle comfortably. Squatting, he watched the half-moon rise, dull yellow and lifeless, wondered whether his disappointment and frustration over the absence of another plane made it seem hotter than it really was.

Questions buzzed annoying as flies. Where had that afternoon's plane come from? Was he on a plane route, or was he near land? Surely he had been drifting too long to still be near South America. Could he be back in the waters off South Africa? Or had the currents taken him north, to America, the Gold Mountain?

The *Benlomond* had been routed for New York after Paramaribo, and the excitement the Chinese crew had felt when they learned they would be going to America had been electric. Though a few of the men had served on ships that docked in New York, not one of them had ever had a chance to go ashore, for the same Exclusion Laws that prohibited Chinese from immigrating to America also denied Chinese seamen the right to shore leave. But America's entry into the war and her need for Chinese seamen had finally forced the Justice Department to give all seamen working on Allied ships the right to shore leave, so the Chinese in the *Benlomond* crew would be able to go ashore legally. Some talked about jumping ship and losing themselves in the small colony of former seamen from Hainan who lived in New York's Chinatown. Others talked of signing articles on American ships where they could earn ten times the wages paid on British ships.

Lim had not planned to do anything other than see the sights, enjoy a woman, and eat as many good Chinese meals as he could afford. But now he pictured himself working for American wages and going home as a Gold Mountain Guest, laden with gifts, rich enough to buy the most elaborate of weddings, lives of ease and plenty for his parents, his bride.

Thoughts of a bath intruded. A body free of dirt and salt in a bed with soft, sweet-smelling sheets. A dinner rich with pork and chicken. Fruit. A pot of steaming, fragrant tea. A cigarette.

The aroma of sulfur from a struck match and the taste of hot, acrid smoke cleansing the odors fouling his mouth spread like a balm through Lim's throat and lungs. He was home. Talking story with all the arch cleverness and drama of a professional storyteller. His hands flew like a puppeteers as he showed the plane circling, diving, landing on the water as smoothly as any bird, then skimming the surface until it reached him.

Breathless with longing, he pulled his knees up against his chest and squeezed as if he could somehow press in his desires. It would all happen just the way he pictured it, he was sure. But when? And how would he endure the wait?

Just before dawn, he heard a plane's engines high and distant. Hoping the hum was real and not imagined, Lim waved in the direction the sound came from, realized the awning was in the way. He clutched a corner pole with one hand, leaned out as far as he dared. A plane burst through a bank of clouds into a pewter sky streaked with pink. He grabbed his flag, stuck it straight out over the side and waved. The sound grew louder, the plane larger, and Lim thrust the oar up and down, swinging it from side to side until the square of canvas took on a frenzied life of its own. But the plane soared on, rapidly fading out of sight.

He dropped the flag onto the deck and kicked it into the well, angry at the plane, the pilot, himself. To the pilot, the raft must be as small as a sesame seed. How would he ever see the flag? He would have to try waving the awning despite the awkwardness. Or at least take it down, making himself and the flag more visible. And with the whole sky open to view, he would be able to maintain a better lookout, respond more quickly when the next plane came.

Jumping over to the opposite deck, he crouched low and tugged at the stiff knots holding the lower corners of the awning. Salt crystals crumbled between his fingers, dissolving in his sweat, vanishing as though they had never existed. Like the *Benlomond.* The men who had served on her. Himself.

Lim shuddered. A fingernail caught in a knot, tore. Cursing, he gnawed the ragged edge smooth so it would not snag again. The chewing activated his saliva and he swallowed. But the tiny quantity of liquid could not ease his thirst or the dull, dry ache lodged like a lump at the back of his throat.

He thought of the dusky gray clouds the plane had burst through and glanced up hopefully. Was the smothering closeness of the last few days finally going to ripen into a squall? Then he shouldn't take down the awning or he wouldn't be able to save any water. On the other hand, if another plane came and the pilot saw him, he wouldn't need it. Either way, with the possibilities of rain and rescue both so close, he could have a proper drink at last.

He reached for the water tank key. But he did not take it down. There was no guarantee that the rain, if it came, would fall over the raft, or that another plane would come. And he had already lost his food and water reserves through overconfidence. All he had left was his life. He selected a vertebra from the tin to chew. There would be no drink, no removal of the awning.

Sucking the dried-out bone gave as little relief as chewing his nail, but a fresh fish would give juice, spinal fluid. He spat out the bone, made a bet. Two.

If he caught a fish, a plane would come.

If he could endure his thirst without dipping into his meager supply of water, the pilot would rescue him.

Using his knife, Lim broke a barnacle off the side of the raft and baited the shorter line that held the smaller hook. Then, setting the flagged oar within easy reach, he lowered hook and line into the sea.

Nothing bit.

For a while he jiggled the line, enticing.

Then, losing patience, he jerked it.

The surface creased with ripples until the area around the line became as wrinkled as the skin on boiled milk. The memory of the pans of milk he had heated to make hot cocoa for the night watch aggravated his thirst, and he regretted all the leftovers he had poured down the drain.

When he held the line still, green water stretched flawless as glass from raft to horizon. Yet Lim sensed a turbulence he could not see that was driving the fish beyond the reach of his hook, and he pulled in the line and exchanged it for the longer one. He hooked the bait securely onto the point of the nail and dropped the line into the sea.

The strange unrest that was driving the fish beyond the length of his lines worried him. The glare burned his eyes. Though it was still early, there was no freshness to the sultry air, no hint of a breeze. He sighed, felt his breath, hot and pungent, blow drops of sweat off his skin, watched them splash, become part of the indolent flop of water against the raft....

Finally there was a tug on the line. He pulled it in. The fish, a three footer, thrashed desperately, but he grabbed it with practiced ease.

He squinted up expectantly at the shimmering haze of heat and glare.

There was no plane.

Why should there be? He had not made a bargain with the Gods, just a bet with himself, a fool's bet.

He hacked off the head and scaled the fish roughly, venting his disappointment, anger, and frustration on the glistening carcass slithering between hands and knife. He sawed the fish in half and pried the bones loose, splitting and then sucking each vertebra. Spinal fluid, flat and insipid, trickled down his throat like water over parched ground, unable to permeate, making real satisfaction impossible. But the dry lump in the back of his throat dissolved and he could swallow easily again.

To get more juice, he slit small pieces of meat and chewed them while cutting and cleaning the fish. He ate the heart and liver, then cut up the rest of the meat for drying, slicing the meat paper-thin to shorten the drying process.

When he finished, he wiped hands slick with blood and offal against his thighs. Stretching belly-down on the deck, he leaned over the side and scooped up water to splash his face, shoulders and chest. Water trickled through the cracks between his fingers. He snatched two tins, plunged them into the sea and poured the contents over his head, repeating the process until his salt-stiff hair was saturated and the gulleys of his face and arms steamed with rapidly evaporating streams of water.

Was he imagining it, or was the sea less smooth? There was no breeze, not enough of a stir to move even a hair. Yet the water seemed darker than the morning. Confused. Almost lumpy. Like porridge. He peered around the awning at the clouds he had seen earlier. They seemed no closer. Could he be near landfall, the beginnings of surf?

Leaping to his feet, Lim examined the horizon on each side of the raft. The few traces of white on the starboard horizon might be clouds or landfall. The greenish blue tint in the sky aft might be the reflection from the shallow water of a lagoon or a reef, or his imagination. Sighing, he thought wistfully of the opera where everything was clear: A good man's face was always red, a bad man's white; ghosts and demons were green, an honest man black; an oar could only mean a boat, a lantern darkness. There were no questions, no doubts, none of the muddle of reality mixed with desires.

Heat changed the bits of white in the sky into snowflakes; loneliness made them birds, the vapor trail of a plane, several planes swarming like dragonflies before a storm.

But they were planes!

Six of them.

"Here! Over here!" he cried, his voice hoarse from yesterday's futile shouting.

As though the pilots had heard his cry, all six planes swerved and flew towards him. Wild with joy, Lim swung the flagged oar over the side, waving and shouting frantically.

The low rumble of engines thundered to a roar, shattering his cries. But the planes, flying high, remained distant as Gods. Between his ribs, Lim's heart beat fierce as the wings of the bird he had trapped: He had to bring down the awning.

Still clutching the flagged oar, he climbed over to the opposite deck, stumbled, grabbed a corner pole. The oar knocked against the strings of drying fish, snagged. He yanked hard, dragging a string loose, scattering strips of fish all over the deck, the canvas, himself. But he was only aware of the pilots, regal and blind as mandarins in silver palanquins, soaring onward, heedless of his cries.

He leaped back to the opposite deck, ripped the metal water tank key from its hemp ties and banged it against the food and water tanks as though he were beating gongs. "Help! Come back! Help!"

High above, the aircraft dipped towards the horizon.

Impossible. They couldn't leave now. Hadn't he won both bets, caught the fish and gone without water?

A low hum broke through his torment. A plane was breaking out of formation, banking around in a slow, easy turn.

Tears streamed down Lim's cheeks, the hard bristles of his beard. Laughing and crying, he lurched from one side of the raft to the other, lashing out with oar and flag, banging the tanks with the water tank key.

The plane grew larger. There was no time to take down the awning, only one way to make himself seen. Awkwardly, he wrapped his arms and legs around a corner pole and shinnied up while wielding oar and flag.

"Here! Over here!"

The plane dropped low and circled, wide at first, then narrower, enfolding the raft in a swirl of vapor trails and noise. Unable to hold on, Lim jumped back onto the deck, slid on a piece of fish, twisting both ankles. Furious at his carelessness, he pulled himself upright. Limping, he kicked aside the scattered fish and string and banged the metal key against the food and water tanks. The plane dipped lower, swamping the raft and Lim's thin cries with its noise.

Struggling back up the pole, it seemed to Lim that if he could only stretch higher, he would be able to see the pilot, feel the hot breath of the engines, even brush a wing tip with the end of his oar. Straining, he thrust the oar out as far as he dared, farther, risking a tumble into the ocean.

"Here!" he pleaded. "Look here!"

The plane waggled its wings. He had been seen!

Then why was it going away?

No, it wasn't leaving. It was turning, coming back. He heard the throttle, a change in the pitch of the propeller, and then it was flying low, swooping like a bird about to make a landing.

Hurling the flagged oar down onto the deck, Lim slid down the pole, flinched at the sting of hard planks against his feet, the sudden buckling of tender ankles when he hit the deck. He crouched, his muscles tensing in anticipation of the plane landing. How close would it come? Would the force of the plane hitting the water knock the raft off balance? How would he get to the plane? Already he could feel the splash of spray, the pitching of the raft as the plane hit the water. He saw himself paddling through churning water, the distance between the plane and himself narrowing, the pilot throwing open the door and pulling him on board.

But wait, the plane was not landing! Instead of hitting the water, its nose was turning up and climbing, disappearing into a cloud. Abruptly it reappeared and then disappeared, flashing in and out of a sudden mist of swiftly moving clouds as it circled the area above the raft. Then it simply hovered.

In the glare, the silver wings glittered harsh as the binoculars of the ship's master three moons before. Was the pilot examining him? Was he to be abandoned once again?

Climbing back up the pole, Lim tried to find identifying markings on the plane's wings, saw none. He slid down, snatched the oar and shook it wildly, pointing at the square of canvas, the white flag of surrender, "Help! I beg you. Help!"

The plane circled again, the white ring it spun binding the raft like a thick, heavy cord. Suddenly it banked and dove toward the water. Blinking back tears of gratitude, Lim bounced back to his feet, saw something jettison from the belly of the plane.

Instinctively, he flinched and backed into the well, yet he could not tear his eyes from the dark object hurtling through the air — until just before it hit the water. Then, eyes clamped shut, he cowered low, bracing himself against the impact, the certainty of death.

He heard a sharp splat, felt the raft pitch and rock, a shower of spray. His fists clenched so tight his nails pierced his palms, he waited for the bomb to explode. All his senses screamed at each new pitch of the raft, each slap of water through the slats, the ominous rumble of engines directly overhead.

There was no explosion.

He peeked cautiously over the side of the well. The canister bobbed harmlessly, and spreading over the water was a shiny, oily substance. Lim looked up at the sky, the plane waggling its wings: There had been no explosion because the pilot had dropped no bomb, but a canister of oil that would smooth the water for a landing.

Hysterical with relief and joy, Lim laughed, waved cheerfully as the plane climbed, vanished behind clouds rimmed with gold.

He waited for it to dive back out of the clouds and land. But it did not. And the only proof that the plane had ever been was the ugly stain spreading over the sea.

CHAPTER TWENTY-THREE

Fighting for control, Lim sank shakily onto the deck.

It was impossible that he would be refused rescue twice. There had to be reasons, good reasons, why the pilot had not tried to rescue him. The plane might not have been the type that could land at sea. Or it might have been low on fuel. Or had a belly full of bombs. So the pilot had chosen a course of action that was safer for them both — dropping a canister of dye to mark the raft, then radioing for help. A special plane or a ship or submarine in the area had probably already picked up the pilot's message and was on its way. And though the pilot would have indicated the raft's longitude and latitude and the dye identified the general area, he should be making himself more visible instead of giving in to despair.

He lashed the flagged oar to the top of a corner pole to give it more height. Then he strung some empty tins together and hung them beneath the flag. Gold streaks of sun caught the parts free of rust, and when he shook them, the metal sparkled bright as signal flashes. But after more than three moons of repeated disappointment, he found it difficult to believe that this time would be any any different. The hollow clatter the tins made reflected his feelings of desolation, reminding him of the melancholy rattles that monks used when begging for succor. He sighed. Monks dedicated their lives to serving the Gods. Yet their pleas for help were often spurned. What then could he hope for?

His ankles throbbed painfully. The suffocating heat squeezed the breath out of his lungs. But he felt too tense to sit. Picking up the fallen lines of fish, he hobbled across the deck, stringing them back up. Perspiration trickled down his arms, irritating. He stopped to scratch, thought he heard the faint wail of a siren.

Heart pounding, his eyes raked the lumpy, gray green ocean stretching beyond the slick of oil surrounding the raft. Nothing. The sky, except for a scattering of clouds, also yawned empty. Swallowing hard, he closed his eyes, hoping he would hear the siren again if he shut out everything else. But with the oil slick flattening the sea, there wasn't even the usual slap of water against the raft.

Using clouds as points of reference, he divided sky and sea into grids for a second, more thorough search. To the west, white clouds converged in an eerie haze that shielded the setting sun like gauze bandages around a clot of blood. Lim's breath caught in his throat. Was that smoke spiralling through the glowing mist?

Afraid the hazy pillars would vanish if he so much as blinked, he stared until smoke, sky, sea, sun, and clouds blurred into a silvery pink shimmer. Curling his fingers into fists, he rubbed his eyes and counted one, two, three, eight ships. A convoy. The Gods and the pilot had not failed him! He was going to be rescued at last!

His skin prickled as hope and caution battled. The convoy would never reach him before dark. But since they had to be aware of his presence, the ships would surely stand by at a safe distance until dawn. But without signals to guide them, the lookouts might miss him. Snatches of breeze were already stirring pockmarks in the shiny dye. And though the air remained heavy and the sea, except for a sullen pulsing, was calm, the raft would drift out of the slick long before dawn....

Dusk became night. As the temperature dropped, a brooding sense of menace smothered the last shreds of hope. Angry with himself, Lim tried to dismiss the low rumbling, the sparks of gold crackling in the darkness where he had last seen the convoy. But memory of the broom star, the Gods' warning of disaster, trampled his efforts, and he fretted over the possibilities — a battle, a storm.

And then, suddenly, he understood his fear. The stifling heat that had caused breezes to die stillborn, the outwardly calm yet deeply disturbed water that had driven the fish beyond reach of his lines, and the cloying humidity that had rotted the strips of drying fish had all been warnings of a storm more deadly than any he had experienced in the past three moons. A storm as menacing as the typhoons which pilloried Hainan.

There, days of thick, oppressive heat were followed by blustery gusts of wind, the startled cries of birds and beasts. Then came the Big Wind itself, shattering tiles, flinging open doors and shutters. Pounding rains swelled shallow streams into raging torrents, ripping trees out of the earth by their roots, gouging out rocks, tumbling mountains and swallowing up mud, animals, people, whole villages. Unsatisfied, the Big Wind might rage for a day or more, ceasing only when its clamorous, unreasoning fury was finally spent.

He remembered how, with the Big Wind's first malicious goadings, families cleared fields and courtyards of tools, drying vegetables, laundry, and animals, shuttering houses and sheds as thoroughly as if they were securing the village against marauding bandits. Nevertheless, rain battered through cracks in bricks, tiles, and shutters, soaking precious stores, while shrieking winds tore off roofs and plundered exposed fields, leaving swathes of death and destruction in their wake.

A Big Wind at sea scoured decks and battened-down hatches with razor-sharp rain and spray. Cargo, straining against lashings, tore loose and crashed against steel bulkheads groaning from the vicious force of pounding waves. Officers and crew, faces gray with exhaustion and worry, battled on the bridge and in the engine room for the life of the ship. While Lim made tea. Great steaming mugs of tea that spilled and scalded as he hurtled through alleyways and fought his way up ladders from galley to bridge.

His role had never struck him before as ridiculous. He was a steward. Serving officers was his job. But now, with lightning flashing bright as rockets at New Year and the awesome rumble of thunder growing louder, he felt as frightened and foolish as a boy about to confront a tiger with bare fists.

Roiling clouds blotted out the rising moon. Wind-slapped canvas cracked like rifle shots. Flinching, he thought of winds tearing off funnels and twisting iron rails, waves so fierce they could break a ship in two. What would they do to the raft, to him?

A sudden blast pitched the raft, jolting Lim into action, and he swiftly stowed hooks, lines, knife, and dipper in the food tank, and empty tins and the water tank key in the compartments. The wind stiffened. The empty tins he had tied to the stanchion clattered. For a moment, the awning billowed like a full sail and the raft scudded effortlessly. Then another blast knocked the canvas in the opposite direction, and the raft shot out of the false calm of the oil slick into swirling hills of dark water.

Clutching his canvas bedding, he abandoned his efforts to secure the raft and tumbled into the relative safety of the well just as a wave washed over the deck, submerging him in churning foam. Before he could catch his breath, another swell buffeted him against the lid of a compartment, the sides of the food and water tanks. Wood and metal lacerated his flesh. Water choked. Coughing and spluttering, he regretted the flag he had slashed so thoughtlessly from the canvas he hugged, wondered if he could still somehow wrap it around three sides of the raft to form a partial bulwark, realized that he had no means of keeping it in place, that there was no time to figure something out.

The series of waves peaked, and he seized the tiny lull that followed to stuff the useless length of fabric into a compartment, tried to think. On board a ship, the metal bulkheads that protected men from the wind and rain and waves of a Big Wind would creak and moan, threatening to break without the skills of officers trained to ride out a storm. And the violence of the battle could shift cargo to one side, causing the ship to list dangerously, even capsize. In a way, the raft's smallness was an advantage, and the slats and metal drums made it buoyant as a cork. No matter how fierce the storm, it would not break, it would not capsize. Like the bamboo groves at home that bent with the wind, it would survive. And so could he.

If he did not panic.

If he managed to stay on the raft.

Angry claws of lightning ripped the sky, revealing swells twenty feet and more from trough to crest. Thunder crashed, exploding clouds, and rain battered the canvas catchment with its weight. Gusts of wind, whistling and hissing, slammed the canvas, knocking the rain water into the sea. Grabbing the slats of decking beneath him, Lim clung to the raft as it swooped up over the spine of a wave and shot over the edge. For a moment, it floated weightless in the air. Then it slammed down hard and spun wildly. Steadying, it coasted deep into a valley, crashing into a fresh wall of water rising out of the depths. Gallons of water poured into the well, and he gasped, choking, until finally the raft rose to ride another swell and he was gulping air.

Struggling against a rising panic more dangerous than any wave, Lim reminded himself of his foolish fright over the first squall, the protection Tien Hau had granted him then. She had brought him through so much. Surely she would not desert him now.

In his awkward crouch, his back soon stiffened. His muscles tensed painfully as he fought to hang on to the bucking raft, and his stomach rose and fell with each new pitch. Afraid he would tire and lose his grip, he thought of tying himself to the raft, remembered he had used all his extra cord to tie the flagged oar to a pole.

Lightning lit up the whole dark sea, leaving it blacker than before. There was an awesome rumble, not just of thunder, but of large, bold combers striking the raft, the roar of even larger breakers coming from afar. Terror tightened Lim's grip on the planks, and he braced himself for the next wave and the next, realized the wind was enforcing a certain rhythm.

He tried to concentrate on the cycles, holding his breath just before one hit so he wouldn't swallow water, relaxing his hold when it receded so he could conserve his strength. For a while, that worked. Then the force of the combers intensified, and they hit with such venom, his fingers were yanked loose and he was hurled against the sharp edges of the metal tanks. Water spewed over the sides and through the slats, and he choked, tasting the sharp bite of salt, blood.

Crawling, he regained his hold near the center of the well just as the next assault struck. His body arched, and he gulped air and water in strangled gasps, fighting nausea, a crazy desire to climb up on the deck. More lightning crackled, and his ears rang with the roar of the wind, the menacing rumble of thunder and booming waves. Screaming winds ripped loose the flag, the awning. The whirling canvas whipped his back. Instinctively he grabbed, pulled part of it down beneath him as the raft plunged into bullying swells determined to make a kill. Solid sheets of water swamped the well, flogging his bruised flesh like merciless whips. Cringing, he drew into himself like a snail into its shell, emptying his head of the cold, the sting of needle-sharp rain and spray, everything, except keeping his hold, his breath, his life....

Sea dragons tossed the raft between them as easily as if it were a sheaf of straw.

Thunder cursed.

Wind shouted encouragement.

Their voices shattered the fragile shell Lim had drawn around him, and he became aware of Monkey stamping across Heaven in his cloud-stepping shoes, sparking lightning with wild slashes of his long iron bar. Then Dragon Lords, their white steeds snorting and foaming, charged across the stormy sea, scattering pearls that exploded like hand grenades under the noses of the enemy. But who among these fickle Gods was his enemy? Monkey, always looking for new mischief? The Sea Dragons sucking his strength like greedy leeches? Or the Dragon Lords swooping in for the kill? Each one was capable of killing or saving him. And, once human, each had knowledge of suffering. But their very humanity made them fallible: gullible, tricky, prone to self-interest. He could not trust one.

Goddesses, kind and generous to each other and the people they served, were more reliable. Like Tou Mou who had taken pity on Miao Shan, the girl whose father had banished her to a nunnery and demanded that she be given all the menial tasks. On Tou Mou's orders, the animal kingdom had helped the girl and so eased her burden. Tou Mou was also capable of walking over waves without getting her feet wet, and it was she, as Goddess of Measure, who must decide the length of Lim's life on earth. If he prayed to her, would she come down from her palace in the Pole Star to smooth out the waters with her many arms? Perhaps, through the third eye in her forehead that allowed her to see everything, she was already aware of his trouble and had dispatched Thousand League Eyes and Favoring Wind Ears, henchmen for Tien Hau, whose spirit had given him the strength to endure this long....

His face and eyes burned. His muscles quivered. His teeth clattered uncontrollably. And still his fingers clung to the planks. Because they were too cold, too numb to be pried loose. Because Tien Hau and her attendants held them there.

Sailors said that if Tien Hau's fire marked the tip of a mast, the vessel and the people in it would survive though the wind was up, the sea high, and everything seemed black. And it seemed to Lim that there was a faint glimmering at the tip of a corner pole. But blinded by a tangled web of wind and rain and spray, he could not be sure.

Parts of the awning that were still loose flogged Lim, searing his skin. Breakers threw up water like dirt for a grave. Spray splattered like gunshot. But he kept his hold on the planks, just as the two Lin brothers had once ridden out a Big Wind by holding fast to a broken mast from their junk which a storm had destroyed. He had seen the temple on Tung Lung Island that the brothers had built for Tien Hau to show their gratitude, and now he vowed that if Tien Hau spared him, he would go to that temple and burn incense in her honor.

Like a miracle, the sea was suddenly and strangely still.

There was no wind, not a breath of air.

Stunned by the abrupt calm and spectral quiet, Lim felt eerily light-headed, unnerved. Muttering his thanks to Tien Hau, he tried to stand, to climb out of reach of the sea washing through the slats of the raft's well, but his fingers, locked to the planks, pinned him down. One by one, he pried them loose, then staggered to his feet.

His feet tangled in the canvas awning crumpled in the well. His legs buckled. He grabbed at the food tank, could not get a grip on the rain-slick surface. Falling, he heard an awful roaring, felt a fierce blast of wind pick up the raft, then fling it down like an angry giant careless with its toy.

Tears of betrayal pricked Lim's eyelids as, once again, the sea became a battleground. Sucking in his breath, he rolled flat on top of the awning and forced his fingers back around the rough planks. Combers churned with redoubled fury, cresting in knifelike ridges that curled and broke in thunderous showers of foam. Rocketing winds shot the raft high onto the crests. Gusts sliced the tops off, plunging him into violent valleys of swirling black water and foam. The force of the rollers scooped the raft back up, and rain and spray whipped from waves pounded his waterlogged flesh.

Gulled by the brief calm, every part of him protested these fresh assaults, and he whimpered for mercy to Kwan Yin, the Goddess who holds the Dew of Compassion in her hand, thought he felt the skirt of her robe brush close. But it was only a corner of the canvas awning billowing in the wind. New swells uncoiled and snapped, and he felt the raft soar up their sides and teeter precariously before pitching into yet another dive.

He concentrated on breathing to the waves' rhythm, praying for an end to the wind, and eventually it did subside. But without the wind's discipline, waves broke in every direction. The raft spun in strange corkscrews between spewing white caps and Lim, unable to keep his grip, lurched from one side of the well to the other, choking, swallowing, and spitting sea water, vomit....

Propped in a corner where the last wave had thrown him, Lim felt like a soggy lump of pain. Separate muscles pranced and jerked beneath bruised flesh. Splinters flecked his palms, his legs. Through a veil of spray and rain, he saw the hint of dirty yellow gray streaks between the tips of waves, the darker clouds just above; and he wondered if this calm was also temporary, another trick of fickle Gods.

Gradually, however, the rain thinned into a soft drizzle and the waves slowly flattened into heaving swells. But inside Lim's head, the storm still raged, and surging waves broke unformed thoughts, numbing, until, finally, there were none.

CHAPTER TWENTY-FOUR

When Lim woke, he was stretched out on a ledge. How or when he had climbed up from the well, he had no idea. Nor did he know how much time had passed since the storm. His eyes caked with sleep, he was aware of burning rays of sun, a hurt more terrible than anything he had experienced before, a thirst so urgent it overrode his pain.

An attempt to sit sent tears spurting down his cheeks. Why was there such intense pain in his groin when he moved? Confused and frightened, he flopped back onto the deck and rubbed away the gritty sleep sealing his eyes.

Blinking against the bright glare of sun, he eased himself up onto his elbows, gasped. The awning lay crumpled in the well. The flag hung limply from the broken oar. String and rotting fish were strewn across both decks. All that could be fixed. And the bruises and scratches covering stiff limbs, belly and chest would eventually heal as they had so many times before. But the genitals swollen twice their size and the strips of skin peeling from puffed up feet. Would they also heal with time? And how would he manage until they did?

Reason told him the Big Wind had blown him far from the convoy he had seen just before the storm. Yet he could not stop himself from searching for it. Dusky clouds hung low near the northwest horizon. Were they the last traces of the storm he had endured or signs of one to come? He sighed, closed his eyes, wanting only to have a long drink of water, then sleep until his body was rested and healed, until rescue came. But his skin, though weathered, was already prickling from the fierceness of the rays beating down. If he did not restore the awning, he would burn.

With his forearm, he pushed aside a snarl of rope ties and rotten fish. Then he leaned down into the well and dragged the awning up on top of him. Water trickled off the scratchy canvas, teasing Lim's thirst, and the taste of bile and salt in his mouth became unbearable. He would have to take a drink before fixing the awning.

Cupping his genitals protectively, he crawled into the well. The effort made him dizzy, slightly nauseated. Distraught that so little activity could make him feel so ill, he denied it by forcing himself to immediately tackle the rope ties latching the compartment where he had stored the water tank key.

The ties, frayed from constant tugging during the storm, broke after a few fumbles. Keeping one hand as a buffer between his genitals and legs and the raft, he lifted the lid with his other. Water gushed out, spilling empty tins, broken glass, the dipper. He rescued the dipper, scraped the broken glass carefully into the sea with the lid of a tin and retrieved the water tank key, his movements slow and awkward because of his position, the use of only one hand.

Wrenching open the water tank required strength he would not have without a rest. But his thirst kept the break brief. He knelt, his knees as wide apart as he could make them and still keep his balance. The lid gave unexpectedly easily, throwing him against the tank. The hot metal scorched. Flipping back, his thighs pinched his genitals, and he doubled over, whimpering.

Water lapped through the slats, whetting his thirst, and as soon as the worst of the pain receded, Lim reached into the tank with the dipper. It splashed swiftly. Relieved there was more water than he remembered, he drank deeply, spat.

The water was as salty as the sea.

Because it was the sea. That was why the lid opened so easily, why the tank was so full. And now, until it rained again or he was rescued, there was no water to drink.

He turned awkwardly to examine the clouds he had seen earlier. Eyes riveted, he willed the ashen blurs to darken, a wind to rise and bring them close, realized he would have to clean out the tank and restore the awning without delay.

Bailing out the water tank while kneeling in the well was exhausting, and he rested, panting like a boxer between rounds, before attempting the awning. Since the two bottom corners did not require him to stand, he did them first, gripping the canvas between his teeth so he could shield his genitals with his hands as he crawled over the slime of old vomit and rotting fish.

He took a long break between corners. But there was no restoration of energy, only the knowledge that if he did not continue, all his previous labor would be wasted. Tiredly stuffing a third corner of the awning between his teeth, he wrapped his arms around a pole and hauled himself upright. His feet were too tender to bear his weight and he leaned heavily against the pole. There was no way he could reach up to the holes at the top, so he tied the canvas at chest level, just high enough to create the slope needed for a makeshift catchment.

By the time he tied the last knot, the sun was dipping close to the horizon. A desultory breeze stirred the clouds, bringing them closer just as he had prayed. But he was too tired, too sore to wash down the canvas, and he persuaded himself that if he slept now he could scrub and bail more effectively when the rain arrived.

Flat on his back, with legs spread wide to avoid pressure on his genitals, Lim felt the full force of the chill night wind, and he wished he had retrieved his bedding from the compartment where he had stuffed it and spread it out to dry while he was working on the awning. The clouds he had seen earlier had vanished without giving rain, and he waited, shivering, for dawn.

He rose with the first smears of light. Though he was still stiff, his genitals and feet seemed less swollen, less tender, allowing him to move a little more easily, to stand briefly, if shakily. But tiny boils scarred his skin which was the color and texture of dried mud.

Climbing into the well to get his fishing tackle from the food tank where he had stored it for safekeeping, he noticed a light film of moisture glistening on the metal. He wet a finger, trailed it across his lips. The bit of dampness seemed to ease his thirst, if only in his mind, and he bent low and licked every drop from both tanks.

The lid to the food tank resisted his first efforts. But when he threw all his weight against it, he heard metal slowly grind against metal, finally twist free. The smell that burst out hit like poison. He knew without looking that the poorly dried fish must have spoiled, and when he reached inside, fish rotted into slime clung to his palms and fingers.

Without water, he would not have been able to eat more than a bite or two of the dried fish. Nevertheless, the loss of all his reserves was shattering, accenting the hunger pinching his belly, the lump of thirst in his throat, and he sank wearily to his knees. But as soon as he could, he felt cautiously in the muck at the bottom of the food tank for his hooks and knife. He found them rusted but usable. Poking them between the slats of the well, he rinsed them clean, then dragged himself back up onto the deck.

Previously a simple task, leaning over the side and prying off a barnacle now required clever engineering, leaving him too winded to exert any control over the water tank key, and it smashed the barnacle, squirting juice all over. Flicking off broken bits of shell, Lim picked up the meat to bait his hook. But the soft bit of flesh between his fingers looked so succulent, he popped it into his mouth instead. He bit down. Fluid seeped out, cool and soothing, but there was only a dribble, not enough to satisfy.

He pried loose another barnacle. This time, unwilling to lose any of the liquid, he tried to break the shell without the water tank key. Smooth, even polished in appearance, the shell was too tough for either his fingers or his teeth. He tried sucking the barnacle whole. Like the seed of a sour plum sucked too long, it hurt the roof of his mouth and his tongue, and he could not get at the meat or the liquid it promised. He spat it out and crushed it with the key.

To draw out the pleasure of tasty juices trickling between his teeth and down his throat, he chewed slowly. Yet it seemed there was only a moment before the lump dried and he swallowed. Feeling cheated, he pried loose and ate all the barnacles large enough to have any meat, then all the ones he could reach without risking a fall.

Glancing worriedly at the sun already high in the sky, he baited his hook with the last bit of meat and cast the line. Harvesting his meal of barnacles had taken longer and been more draining than he realized, and there was still so much to do. Some of it, like cleaning the decks and food tank and fixing the flag, he could put off. But other chores had to be taken care of without delay. The fish he caught would have to be cleaned, the lines for drying retied. And he could not pass another night without bedding.

He pulled in the line and transferred the bait to the larger hook. There wasn't enough good fishing time left to follow his usual routine of catching a small fish and using it as bait to catch a large one. And a small fish would not give him the liquid he needed even more than meat.

Half crouching, half sitting, he cast the line. After a while, he stood, leaning heavily against a corner pole. Then he knelt. No position was comfortable, and he could not keep any position for long. Was that why the fish weren't biting, because he was too restless? Or was the barnacle too small to disguise the hook? Or had the storm driven the raft into a desert patch?

It had happened before, when his food tank had been well stocked with dried fish, and he had not really worried, confident that before his supply ran out, the raft would drift again into an area rich with fish. Even now he would not be so anxious if he had water, if the absence of fish did not suggest the possibility of another storm.

The sky was cloudless, the sea flat, but hadn't it been just as clear, just as calm before the Big Wind? His confidence eroded, he fretted, unable to decide whether he should continue to fish, though he rarely caught anything in the afternoons, or take care of his other chores.

Turning the water key had peeled off calluses softened by long soaking during the storm and the fishing line bit into the tender flesh beneath. Finally, afraid he would break his skin if he worried the line any longer, he pulled it in and ate the bait. Then, his movements sluggish as if he were drugged, he dragged the bedding out of the compartment.

Rust and mildew stained the soaked canvas in huge blotches, and he spread it out on the ledge to dry, stretched out beside it for a brief rest. Instead he sank into a deep sleep, waking only once to crawl beneath the folds of the canvas to escape the cold night wind.

The day before, the condensation on the two metal tanks and the meal of barnacles had blunted Lim's thirst into a burning irritation. But today there had been no relief. Warm and dry under his bedding, he slept late into the morning so that any moisture that might have dampened the raft had evaporated by the time he woke, and his tongue gorged his throat like an overstuffed liver sausage. Searching for a barnacle for bait, he discovered a few clumps of moss-like growth. He scraped off a handful and stuffed it into his mouth. But the greenish mess, saturated with salt water, made him more thirsty, and when he finally found a barnacle he could reach without danger, he sucked the meat dry before baiting the hook.

Now his empty belly shot cramp-like pains to his shoulders, the base of his spine, and he wondered if eating raw fish had given him worms after all. He also questioned whether he had misjudged the water in the water tank as too tainted to drink, if he had mistaken the disaster the broom star foretold. When the Big Wind hit, he had assumed that was the calamity the Gods had threatened. Now he wondered if they had been warning him against his arrogance in thinking he had conquered the sea.

Crouched precariously on the edge of the deck, Lim felt the sun boring into his skull. Exhaustion pressed his back into the stoop of an old man, and he yearned to lie in the well of the raft where cooling water would lap his aching limbs, calm his twitching muscles, and soothe his fingers, which were rubbed raw from playing the line. There would also be more shade and less dehydration.... But his feet and genitals, still puffy and tender, might swell again, and the clusters of saltwater boils would grow. His mouth twisted into a bitter grimace. What difference would that make if he didn't catch a fish soon or rain didn't fall?

Despite what he thought were worms agitating in his belly, it wasn't food he needed so much as liquid. Worms or no, he could probably endure half a moon without food. But how much longer could he last without water? Though the heat was fierce, he could not sweat. His throat was so parched he could not swallow. And he was only urinating once a day instead of the two or three times when he was on full rations.

Thinking of his urine, the arc of golden liquid falling into the sea, Lim's throat opened with desire. The gold and silver sea gleamed cruelly seductive and he shook his head to break its call. Drinking salt water meant certain death, all seamen knew that, whereas drinking urine...

As far as he could remember, that had never been discussed.

He combed his memory.

The shimmering below him became the shimmer of maggots crawling over the huge clay urns where villagers released their bladders and bowels, saving the urine and feces to spread over the fields to renew the life of the tired, overused soil. He had been terrified of the maggots the first time he had teetered on the lip of the tub. But filled with pride at being considered old enough to use it at last, he had swallowed his fear.

Babies and little children that might fall into the tub wore split-bottomed pants so they could relieve themselves anywhere, and puppies ate their droppings. They were always puppies because, having nothing else to eat, they died before they were full grown.

Was that the answer? That drinking his urine would kill him? But the puppies often lived as long as six months, sometimes more. And he would not be eating his feces. Besides, he would only drink his urine once, maybe twice, before he caught a fish, or rain fell, or rescue came.

He thought of the exiles banished to Hainan. Repelled by the conditions and the people around them, they had all died or killed themselves. Except one. Unlike the others, that man had accepted the facts of the life he must lead, forcing himself to eat suspect flesh and crude root vegetables.

Lim's bladder throbbed, urging release. Still he resisted. As he had resisted eating fish until he had exhausted his rations. As he had resisted eating it raw. But yesterday he had eaten barnacles, and that morning he had stuffed his mouth with moss just as the village leper crammed down grass and mud when begging brought no food....

He pulled in the line. Hoping the bit of meat would not become too shriveled to tempt a fish when he cast the line again, he coiled the line with the bait still on the hook. Then he pulled himself upright. His legs, numb from remaining too long in one position, would not support him, and he hugged a corner pole, relieved he had an excuse to delay, yet impatient also as tingling waves rippled down thighs, calves, and feet, restoring circulation.

Finally, he was able to stumble into the well, to find a tin. He did not have the strength to stay on his feet, so he sat on the edge of the deck, one hand gripping the edge and the other holding the can, both feet flat on the bottom of the raft's well, bracing.

Nothing came.

Thoughts of clear water drawn from a well being poured into clay jars, the gurgle of a faucet, and a waterfall made his thirst worse.

Was he trying too hard?

Or was it too late?

The possibility that he might not be able to create urine magnified Lim's longing. He thought regretfully of all the water he had ever wasted, especially the excess rain water he had tipped out of the canvas catchment so often. And he wished he had drunk his fill of the water in the tank before the storm hit, that he had not been in such a hurry to clean out the tainted water....

A drop, luminous as dew, emerged, fell into the can.

"Shhhhh," he crooned like a mother coaxing a baby. "Shhhhh."

And another drop fell.

The unsteady drip, drip revived a story Lim's father told about a family that had escaped to the hills during war in ancient times. That family, seeking refuge in a cave, had been sealed in by a fallen boulder. They had dug desperately for days. But escape proved impossible, and they resigned themselves to sitting and waiting for rescue, knowing they would surely die when they exhausted their supply of food.

Then one day they noticed a turtle that had been in the cave from the beginning, only it had been so still, they thought it a rock. Anxious to discover how it managed to survive, they studied the turtle. And in the next few days, they saw its head slowly protrude then shrink back into its shell, its tongue stretching out occasionally to catch a drop of water dripping from the rocky clefts above.

Without food or any other hope, the family imitated the turtle.

Eight-hundred years passed before they were discovered. But when the boulder was rolled back, the family was alive.

It was a story only, one of many that people like his father told to give themselves hope, the courage to endure. But lost in it, Lim's twin needs to drink and urinate became one, and when the story was over, he found he held almost half a can of warm, lemon yellow liquid in his hands.

CHAPTER TWENTY-FIVE

The stench in Lim's mouth was so rank he could neither smell nor taste the urine. But he could feel each sip dissolve the salt on his lips, stinging the cracks, then roll, biting, on his parched tongue before sliding, painful as a sword, down his throat.

Bit by bit, saliva returned. And he no longer felt he was going to choke. But the relief was short-lived.

All too soon he felt thirsty again, the fierce burning in his throat worse than before. He felt sucked dry, overheated, not unlike the times he had become ill from eating poisoned fish. Could his body already be reacting to the poison in his urine? Or was he simply feeling the heat more because of his thirst, because he could not sweat?

He lowered the broken oar and flag into the sea and covered his face with the square of wet fabric. Under the scorching rays of afternoon sun, it dried quickly and again each breath seared his nostrils, his throat. He rolled over onto his side, grimacing as fleshless bones rubbed against the edges of his canvas bedding, and lowered the canvas back into the sea.

The cycle repeated itself like the cycle of questions in Lim's head. Was the gnawing in his belly from worms? Was he better off drinking his urine or trying to go without? He was losing his strength so quickly, would he have enough left to bring in the fish when he caught it, to bail when it rained, to wave and shout when rescue came?

The questions, the heat, his thirst, and the need to soak and resoak the canvas ground relentless as millstones, and by the time the night wind finally stirred, he could barely drag the bedding over himself.

He was trawling for fish, but there were none, so he dove overboard to search for them. Skillfully, he plunged deeper and deeper until he found them, all the fish in the sea, cavorting in a huge basket woven with hundreds, thousands of green willow twigs. A pilot fish with seven dark rings circling its body swam close, showing him the entrance, and already glorying in the catch he would make, Lim followed it in — remembering too late the basket was a fisherman's snare that allowed fish to enter, but not to leave.

A junk filled with fresh fruits sailed close. He could hear the vendor calling out to the housewives in the sampans, "Come and buy! Peaches the size of footballs! Watermelons that melt into sugar in your mouth!" The vendor's cleaver sliced through the jade green rind of the watermelon and sticky pink juice dripped from the blade and the chopping block into the sea.

Choked with longing, Lim battled the raft through a swarm of sampans to the junk, only to find when he reached it that he had no money to pay.

Red sky dissolved into orange pink and then blue. A half mile west of the raft, clouds gathered. He could smell the dampness of the coming squall, feel the cool cleansing wash of rain over the raft, hear the bubble of beautiful clear water spilling over the canvas catchment and water tank.

But when he opened his eyes, stars crowded a sky bright with moonlight and he could not see a single cloud.

The spirits of the dead crew pinned Lim onto a bed of bamboo stakes and poured molten copper down his throat while the bird he had snared plucked out his eyes and tongue. Slowly, a bell descended over them all. The heat intensified, and the stink of blood and burning flesh became overpowering. Lim clawed at the bell, fighting to hold it off. But like the hot blue flame on a gas burner, the bell had no substance, only the ability to hurt.

In the morning, Lim's belly was tender to the touch, his mouth dry and foul. And his skin, wrinkled as an old man's, had become more gray than brown. Wherever it flaked, it was rough with cracks. Sores wept. A strange, reddish rash covered the backs of his hands, his swollen feet and ankles. Pus oozed from a cluster of broken saltwater boils.

Fear that he had cheated the sea only to have his body die piece by piece sapped any energy the night of thin, restless sleep might have restored. Yet something inside him, some inner force made him go on, and he took down the fishing line. Relieved he had thought to leave the bait on the hook the day before, he sagged against a corner pole and dropped the line into the sea.

He closed his eyes, thought wistfully of the previous moon when fishing had brought peace, even pleasure, and he had known a measure of physical comfort and contentment as master of the raft, his fate. It had been an illusion, he realized, now that his water and food tanks were empty, his body painfully and visibly rotting. There was no mastery, no escape from the cycle of life where the sorrows of men are the return of their own evil acts in former lives.

According to the monks, a man who kills too many animals lives out an incarnation riddled by disease; a man who snatches baby animals from their mothers is punished by painful separations from his future family. What would they say he had done to warrant his current suffering? Or was the nightmare about his shipmates real? Had they really become evil spirits seeking vengeance because he had lived when they had died?

He was not afraid of death. All life was a march towards it, and he believed what he had been taught, that birth was not a beginning, nor death an end. But if he died now, without sons to feed his spirit, the hunger and thirst he was suffering would be his lot for all eternity, and that he could not bear.

The salt crusting Lim's beard and hair itched, and he scratched his jaw and scalp, showering his arms, his sunken chest and legs with salt and scaly skin.

Dead skin.

Death...

Were the men on the other raft dead? Or had they been rescued, or found a way to sail to land? What would five men in his current situation do? Turn on each other? Draw lots? Or kill the weakest among them in order to eat his meat and drink his blood?

Scattered high in the sky were a few tattered clouds, their movements sluggish and desultory as his musings. If the three closest bits drifted together and became one, rain would fall, Lim promised, scowling up at them, willing them to obey.

The glare of the sun shriveled his eyeballs, forcing his eyes shut again, and he was suddenly, wonderfully, walking down the street of a market town at festival time, his nostrils quivering from the delicious aromas of the food stalls. Sizzling squares of bean curd stuffed with pork. Noodles in a pot of broth so rich it swam with islands of fat. Too starved to wait politely to be served, Lim plunged his hands into the soup and grabbed the noodles. They slipped through his fingers, and he cried his disappointment, his bitterness so intense he jerked awake.

Just in time, he caught hold of the fishing line sliding out of his grasp and yanked it onto the raft. Reeling from fear, relief, and dizziness, he clutched the line and hook to his chest, paralyzed by what might have been, what could still occur. Then, as the waves of panic receded, he tried to think. But the stifling heat, the squirmings in his belly, and the swollen lump of thirst gorging his throat smothered reason.

He struggled to sit, to coax out a can of urine. It came slowly, in dribbles and squirts between long pauses. Darker, thicker than the day before, there was also less. Again the pungent, steaming liquid burned the sores on his lips. But, for a little while at least, it also broke the thick cobwebs clogging his mouth and throat, dulling his thirst, quieting the spasms in his belly.

He cast the line. Though he could not stop the trembling in his fingers or the sudden quivers rippling through his arms and legs, the shock of almost losing his hook and the knowledge that he had no strength to pry loose another nail held Lim's attention. For a while. But as the sun reached its peak and the heat intensified, the heavy air clamped down like a coffin lid and again his thoughts drifted.

Marshalling all his forces, Lim counted numbers from zero, promising a plane would come if he could reach one hundred. But the numbers kept running from him until they were so hopelessly jumbled he could not remember where he had ended or should begin.

He tried a different approach, something easier that assured more immediate satisfaction: If he played the line instead of just letting it dangle, he would catch a fish.

But his fingers twitched, snarling the line, and his attempts to untangle it made it worse.

Afraid a large fish might pull the line taut and snap it, Lim had been careful never to tie the line to the raft before. Now he acknowledged that he was more likely to lose hook and line if he did not, and he knotted the end of the line around the corner pole before casting the hook back into the sea.

Prior to the storm, Lim had often had to remind, even force himself to eat. Now, on his fifth day without food, he could think of nothing else. Special festival dishes, food from the different countries he had visited, even shipboard meals wafted before him, their remembered fragrances and tastes driving him mad.

He scooped out the slime in the food tank, searching each handful of putrid flesh for something edible to appease the gnawing in his belly. And though he had known the project was hopeless from the start, his whole body convulsed in a long, deep shudder of disappointment when he could not find even one tiny scrap.

He jiggled the fishing line dangling from the corner pole, and in the swirling eddies Lim thought he saw the skeletons of ships filled with juicy oranges from Haifa, fragrant ripe bananas, carcasses of tender meat, cascading grain.

Phantom pilots scrawled words in the sky, promises of rescue if he did as they instructed. Voices softly echoed the words, "Swim. You can swim to land. Swim." The whispers grew louder, more insistent, and he wanted to obey.

A tug on the line snapped the spell. A fish at last! Drawing it in, he felt a lack of weight. But a small fish was better than no fish. There wouldn't be much liquid in the vertebrae. But he could chew the meat for the juice, and the kidneys and liver and heart would be moist.

There was no fish.

There was also no bait.

Pushing down his disappointment, he dragged himself from one side of the raft to another, searching for a barnacle he could reach, something, anything that would tempt the fish that had eaten his bait. When he found none, he gathered the remnants of his strength to play the line, substituting guile for bait. But no fish came near the empty hook and he began to wonder if he was really out of the desert patch, or if the shriveled bit of bait had simply disintegrated and fallen off the hook.

White fur coated his teeth, the sores on his lips, his tongue. Ulcers speckled his gums. Suspecting they came from drinking urine, he had delayed giving in to his need to drink, hoping it would rain or he would catch a fish. Somehow, he had endured through the worst of the noonday heat. But he could deny himself no longer.

Lacking the energy to move from where he slumped next to the corner pole, he simply crept closer to the edge and dangled his feet over the side. For safety, he hugged the pole with one arm, held a can in place with his other.

A few drops trickled agonizingly slowly into the can.

Too thirsty to wait for more, Lim gulped the dark, thick drops in a single sip. Then, staring down at the sea, he waited for more.

Water licked the raft, his toes, the musical ripples calling softly, urging him to trust himself to the gentle swells, to lie still and let them rock him. Mesmerized by the dreamy motion, the can slid out of his hand and tumbled into the sea's welcoming embrace.

He wanted to weep for the urine lost to the sea. But he could no longer make tears. Half squatting, half sitting, he held another can, waited anxiously for more.

His arm tired.

He switched the can to the other hand, then back again.

He coaxed.

He crooned.

But no urine came.

Panicked, he scoured the sky for clouds, saw none. Neither was there any sign of ship or plane or land.

During the night, the white rabbit in the moon ground rice. The white powder drifted down from the sky, becoming moonbeams Lim's mother promised to cook into a magic gruel to celebrate his return. But why did she delay when he needed the magic now?

Hunger and thirst ripped large holes in the black sea of his mind. And stars leaped through the jagged tears, their colors flaming bright as they blazed wild, erratic trails that fizzled into nothingness, the nothingness he would become if he did not eat soon.

His mother pointed to a wasp that was tearing a leg off a grub trapped in the same jar. The wasp offered the broken leg to the grub. The grub ate it. Was his mother telling him to do the same?

The only possible food was himself, and he sawed a piece from his thigh. The pemmican tin knife was blunt. Yet he felt no pain. And though there was no fire to cook the meat, it tasted delicious.

Lim chewed slowly, savoring the blood and juices lubricating his throat. But a single slice was not enough to fill his belly. So he carved and ate another piece.

And then another.

Until there was nothing of him left.

And still he was not full....

His mother said that for every person in this world, there shines a star in the sky. The bigger stars are persons of importance, the smaller ones common folk. When an important person dies, his star shoots to the earth as a meteor. But a common person's star fades unobserved like the ones dimming before the dawn. Was one of these stars his?

Scarcely breathing, Lim watched the sky streak pink, then yellow and red, and finally blue. The last star vanished. He remained. But was he alive?

Torpor weighted his limbs, pinning him to the deck, and though he knew that any moisture condensed on the metal tanks would soon evaporate, he could not move. Inside his mouth he felt a sticky dampness. Sucking, he tasted blood from loosened teeth, his gums. He tried to swallow, but it hurt too much and the activity stirred the worms in his belly. Even lying still he could feel them gnawing his flesh like the white ants in Hainan devoured furniture, their silent, invisible chewing so relentless that only broken splinters remained of what had once been good and whole.

Groaning, he dragged himself across the deck towards the film of dampness glistening on the water tank. He licked feebly. The trace of moisture on his tongue aggravated his thirst and he slumped against a corner pole gasping like a beached fish.

As clearly as if they were beside him now, Lim saw the fish heaped inside his father's baskets. Their eyes dulled. Blood oozed between the tiny teeth rimming their mouths. Yet they clung to life, their little mouths opening and closing ever more slowly as they gradually suffocated to death....

He examined an abscess on his thigh, the cluster of saltwater boils near the heel of his left leg, the festering sores on his arms, another abscess on the elbow. If he did not lance and clean them, their poison could kill him as surely as the lack of rations.

Reaching up to get his knife from the corner pole, his hand shook like the last leaf of autumn. How could he trust it? How could he not? Caught between need and fear, Lim felt a searing flash of envy for those who had died when the torpedoes struck.

A never-ending tumble of sharp golden spears plummeted from the sun into the sea. Eyes closed against the brutal glare, Lim lay on the canvas bedding spread over the deck, straining to hear the flip-flop of a fish's fin striking the raft's bottom, to feel a tug on the line he had twined around his fingers. But the only sound was the incessant lisp of water he could not drink, a painful gurgle of gases in his belly.

Long and monotonous, the afternoon wore on. The sun inched towards the horizon, and slowly, slowly, another day crawled to a close. The deep red sun sank into the sea, locking him into a darkness as harsh and forbidding as the grave. Lim pinched himself cruelly. As intended, pain crackled through sunken hollows, the false flesh of swellings that bound his stiffened joints. Whimpering, he embraced the fevered thrusts, pain his only weapon now against the sleep he must fight if he was to succeed in this struggle against death. For he knew that once he surrendered he would never waken. Then his bones would bleach clean and white as the fish skeletons that had decorated his raft, and his life would be no more than the phosphorescence shimmering all around him, a momentary glitter that vanished with the bright light of day.

As the last sparks of hurt faded into a dull, familiar ache, Lim's dry, cracked lips sagged into the caricature of a yawn. He tried to stifle it. To speak. Sing. Create a noise that would beat back sleep. But no sound came. Weary beyond measure, his eyelids drooped shut and he was a boy again, watching his mother make paste out of a basket of shrimp his father brought home from the sea. Placed live into a huge jar with just enough salt to keep them from spoiling, the shrimp digested themselves, the jar a purplish hiss of agitated self-destruction.

The salty sting of the cold night wind brought him back to the raft. The moon, almost three-quarters full, had risen, bathing the sea in its ghostly light. Stars danced like fiery suns, the ones flaming in his head burning the brightest and fiercest. Something dark and feather soft brushed his cheek. The death crane come to carry him across the yellow river?

His fingers twisted his flesh weakly, forcing a renewal of raw pain, proof of life. He heard a shrill, childlike cry. Puzzled, he touched his lips, felt the scratch of a chicken's feet stumbling across his own. Was it One Eye coming to punish him for eating her?

He remembered how the rare fragrance of cooked meat and the sounds of sucking and gnawing had proved too tantalizing. Tears running down his cheeks, he had eaten the choice pieces his mother had picked for him.

"But I was only a child...." His mouth opened but no sound came out. He felt the sharp jab of a beak in his shoulder. His arm lashed out feebly, grazing the tips of feathers, flapping wings, and another shrill cry shattered the night.

He thought he saw a bird, small and black, hovering just above his head, its wings gleaming in the moonlight. A magpie, the first of all the magpies in the world, coming to build a bridge between him and his betrothed?

Moonglow dappled the water, revealing flashes of white flitting erratic and ghostly. But magpies were black, like the bird landing lightly on the raft, less than a foot from the fingers of his right hand.

It eyed Lim quizically, hopped a little closer, and he saw the bird for what it was — a means to life.

He dared not make a grab for it until he was sure he would succeed.

He dared not wait lest the bird flew away.

Finally, concentrating everything he had on keeping his hands steady, he reached out, trembling from lack of food, a longing to stuff the bird into his mouth, feathers, claws and all.

He caught both legs, scrawny and rough.

The bird struggled, cried, and pecked wildly. But it was too small to be any match for even Lim's feeble strength. Grasping its wings, he caged it shakily with both hands and swung down, knocking the bird's head against the deck.

Once. Twice. A third time.

Bone cracked. Crunched. Became a dull thud.

There was the sound of Lim's harsh breaths, the throb of the sea; a faint flutter, imagined or real.

For a moment he stared at the bird blankly, the pulpy mass where head had been. Then he took his knife, sawed a deep slit into the still warm flesh at the base of the neck just above the breast.

As though the bird were a mug, he lifted the body to his dry, broken lips and squeezed and sucked the slit with the last of his strength. Thin, watery blood trickled down the sandy desert of his throat. Gradually it thickened. Clots coated his tongue and throat like a salve, and he tasted it, sweet and strong. Like liver.

The blood sharpened his appetite, and he tore off a handful of feathers and sank his teeth into the bird. Sore and loose, his teeth barely grazed the skin. He fumbled wearily for his knife, hacked a hole just large enough to worm in two fingers and drag out the intestines. He squeezed out the partially digested food and waste in tiny dribbles which he sucked like an old man, resting, almost dozing, between swallows. Then he extracted and cut the heart and liver and kidneys into soft, moist bits he could eat without chewing.

He rested, scraped off a bit of the skin with his knife, chipped off a scrap of meat, sawing through the tissues anchoring it to the bone. He ground it slowly between his teeth, rested, cut and chewed another snippit, and then another.

The moon dipped close to the horizon. His eyelids drooped heavily. Blood from his gums mingled with the bird's. His jaws ached. But the pain and blood created an almost voluptuous pleasure, and he gnawed the fragments of meat, then sucked the marrow out of the bones until all that was left were feathers, a few scraps of skin, the scattered shards of hollowed bone.

CHAPTER TWENTY-SIX

The next morning Lim baited his hook with scraps of skin from the bird, cast the line with renewed hope. There had been moments of delirium in the previous day or two when he thought he might have died and was going through the stages of hell and did not know it. Now he wondered if the Gods might have been putting him through a series of tests he did not recognize or understand.

Before his father was permitted to start a martial arts school in a village, the head man would test his skills by challenging him to a fight. Only when defeated would the head man acknowledge Lim's father's mastery, his right to train villagers in defense skills for a fee. Was the bird an acknowledgment that Lim had passed his tests? Or was it a sign of the Gods' forgiveness?

His mother insisted that, "High Heaven never betrays the wretched," and to prove her point, or to convince herself, she spoke often of the Dragon King who had parted the waters of the ocean to save a drowning man, the Goddess who had stopped the floods that threatened to drown all mankind by patching the holes in Heaven's floor. Was that why the bird had come when there had been nothing to attract it? Because the Gods, though sometimes angry or capricious or neglectful, were never malicious? Or was he alive simply because the number of years allotted him by Tou Mou, the Goddess of Measure, had not been used up?

He did not know the answer to this new riddle any more than he had understood how he had succeeded in resurfacing and swimming back to the raft the time he had fallen overboard. But he was sure that the bird, like that incident, was also a turning point.

As though to confirm it, a soft warm drizzle fell shortly before noon. With the sun poking through the few thin clouds almost as soon as the shower began, there was no time to wash the canvas catchment, no chance to bail. Neither did he have the strength to do either. There was so little water in the trough of the awning that he could not fill the measure without tilting the canvas, and the few mouthfuls he sipped were tainted with salt and dirt. Nevertheless, the water cleared his mouth and throat and strengthened his hope. And though no fish bit, he was confident more rain and more birds would come.

The sky changed from hammered gold to a brilliant, bloody russet. Looking at the bright red light reflected in a thousand dancing pinpoints on the sea, Lim relived the pleasure of blood, thick and warm, coursing down his throat, the satisfying rip of flesh from bone, and he searched the radiant sky for dark smudges, the silhouettes of birds.

He tried squatting in readiness. But his legs were too weak to support him for long. So he half knelt, half sat, leaning against a corner pole. Tense as a drawn catapult, he felt like the man in a photograph he had once seen of a prisoner forced to stand on tiptoe behind a pointed stake. So long as the prisoner maintained his guard, he was safe. But if he relaxed for even a moment, the stake would pierce his gullet.

Remembering, Lim fretted that he had been too quick to declare his new victory, that the bird and the shower were a new and exquisite form of torture rather than a reprieve. The cries of the bird he had killed might have frightened the others away. Or perhaps there was only the one bird he had already caught and eaten....

Sky and water darkened. Stars leaped into faint light in every part of the sky. Phosphorescence speckled the violet'black sea. But a bank of clouds hid the rising moon, and if there were any birds, Lim could not see them.

Flecks of phosphorescence broke, came together.

Stars shrank and then brightened.

Dark shadows danced just above the surface of the water.

He eased back into a crouch, discovered his legs had gone to sleep. He massaged them in a fever of impatience, heard the soft swish of wings, felt the faint, playful flick of water. Calves and thighs still tingling, he squatted shakily.

His eyes darted from sea to sky, back to the sea.

Feathers rustled drily.

He steadied himself, heard the delicate patter of feet on the opposite ledge. Not daring to move any more than absolutely necessary, he arced his head back hair by hair. But with most of the moon still veiled by clouds, he saw only the gleam of canvas awning though he could hear the quick stabs of a beak.

Glad now for the clouds shielding the moon, Lim pressed his fingers down hard against the deck to keep his balance and rotated a few more inches, saw two flashes of white. Was there more than one bird?

Were it not for the spots of white on its head or rump, he could not tell which, the bird would have remained hidden. And even now, without the tap tap of the beak, he would have thought it a fantasy. Was he as invisible to the bird? To catch it, he would have to turn around entirely, and he debated whether he had the control necessary to continue his slow, cautious swivel.

Suddenly the pecking turned into agitated bickering. So there was more than one bird! The white spots fluttered, exploding into flight. Instinctively he threw himself in the direction of the birds taking wing, landing in a painful, sprawling heap across both decks, one leg in the well. Shrill cries and the flap of wings shattered the night. But beneath his chest he felt feathers, the sharp beak of another bird.

Unlike the birds that had come to the raft before, the two Lim had caught and eaten seemed too small and delicate to survive in the open sea, and the following day, while he fished, he searched the horizon on every side for sign of land. He found none. Neither did he catch any fish. Discouraged, he dozed, dreamed he was a baby safely cradled in his mother's arms.

She dipped a cloth into a basin of warm water and wiped his forehead and cheeks. Moisture dampened his eyes and nose and mouth, and he crowed with pleasure. His mother wet the cloth again and water trickled into his ears, his nose, tickling, then swamping, so that he could not breathe.

He coughed, struggling for air. Arms flailed, and he woke to rain coming down in torrents, spilling into his eyes, his nose, his mouth. He was too weak to risk climbing up onto the ledge to wash the awning. But the downpour seemed hard enough to slough off the worst of the dirt and salt. Kneeling in the well, he punched the slope of the awning to empty the trough when it filled. Once. Twice. A third time. Then he crawled over to the side, dunked his head into the trough and gulped the trapped water. It tasted sweet. But his stomach revolted at the sudden riches, and he brought the water back up. Frightened, he did not drink more. But he swilled out the tank and bailed, and as he staggered between awning and water tank, rain dribbled down his gaunt cheeks in grubby rivulets, washing his sores.

That night, there were no birds. But when he cast his line the following morning, he discovered he was back in waters thick with fish. Though he fished with the smaller hook and the fish he landed weighed less than a pound, he was exhausted after catching only two.

After the birds, the white, flaky fish were a treat, easy to cut up and chew. The organs had a wonderful flavor, and the red meat just under the fins of the little brown fish tasted like tenderized beef. But he knew from throwing up the water that his shrunken belly would accept only small quantities of food and he ate only one, hanging the other up to dry.

The return of fish as well as rain brought a relief of tension that was enormous. He slept long and deeply, ate and drank increasingly large amounts. Within a few days, his hands were steady enough for him to lance his abscesses. But breaking through the hard shell to the suppuration festering beneath, pressing out the poison, and cutting off the bits of putrefying skin was so wearying that he was forced to recognize that his return to health would take far longer than the rapid deterioration he had experienced.

Moving slowly, he cleaned up the raft bit by bit. Scraping the rust off his knife and hooks and bailing tin and repairing his lines were the most important tasks, so he did these first. They were simple chores he normally sandwiched into odd moments. Now they required whole afternoons. Picking up the ties that had broken and fallen during the storm consumed an entire day, re-braiding and stringing them up took three. But the work kept him from thinking, and he could do a little more with each passing day.

One by one his sores healed. His boils and rashes disappeared. The swellings in his joints shrank. He was strong enough to fish with the larger hook again, to catch three or four birds in a single night. Rain fell almost daily, keeping the level of the water tank steady. With more food and fresh water than he needed, his ability to sweat and expel waste returned, and he no longer looked or felt like a skeleton encased in skin.

He scoured the food tank, cleaned and aired out the compartments and restored the awning. The stink of rot vanished, and the raft looked almost as it had before the storm. Sun and salt had bleached the planks silver. Pacing, wind, and spray had worn them smooth except where chipping and banging from the heavy water tank key marred. Nailheads punctured the planks, the rusted ones brown orange like cigarette burns, and rusty brown streaks stained the canvas awning.

So familiar had it all become that Lim had to struggle to imagine a time when he had not been on the raft, burned up by the sun, chilled by the night, half drowned by rain, constantly searching for food, catching then eating it, all the time watching warily for danger. And though he clung to the belief that he would some day go home to his parents and wed his betrothed, his memories seemed a long time ago and not at all important, his future equally distant and unreal.

Drying meat only for reserves, he had less work and more time to fill. To amuse himself, he tried catching the birds in different ways. They seemed to fly tirelessly for amazing lengths of time and they pattered easily over swells on their tiny webbed feet. But they could not walk across the deck without the support of their wings, and he played at stalking them, then grabbing their legs. Sometimes he tried catching them with his fishing line, floating a baited hook on the surface where they fluttered, pecking at creatures too small for him to see.

He experimented more daringly with food. Looking for marrow, he discovered many of the birds' bones were hollow, and when he carefully picked apart a skeleton, he saw the hollow bones in the wings were connected to their lungs, allowing them to fill with air. These he used as straws to suck out the clear fluid surrounding a fish's tiny brain, pretending he was drinking the white of egg. He crunched the eyes of fish as though they were lumps of barley sugar. And he ate the granular masses of yellowish tissue he sometimes found behind a fish's swimming bladder, finding they tasted like roe.

Flaccid livers, chewy kidneys, crunchy marrow, fatty skin, creamy brains, birds' blood, and fish's spinal fluids offered a variety of tastes and textures. The birds' antics provided entertainment. Yet the world into which the storm had flung him seemed bleaker, more desolate and dreary. For he realized now that like an animal plucked from its home and caged in a zoo, he would never be a part of the world around him, and he lived at the mercy of his keepers.

CHAPTER TWENTY-SEVEN

For four days there were heavy showers. There was no storm. Not even a wind. Only rain. The kind Lim had prayed for less than a moon before. Steady. Relentless.

His skin, tender from the constant wetness, felt sodden as a sponge. His bones ached. His joints and genitals and feet swelled, and he felt a tingling numbness in his legs, a chill despite the heat.

Finally, the downpours slackened, and the sun returned each day in bright clear dawns. But clouds gathered by mid-morning, and most afternoons there were showers of hard, driving rain, sometimes a squall. Even when there was no rain, the air dripped moisture. And though Lim's skin might unwrinkle and the swellings shrink, the canvas awning he depended on as a catchment had no such healing powers and it stank of mildew. How long before it disintegrated?

Since meat spoiled before it could dry, Lim no longer cut the fish into strips. But birds were so plentiful that he did not need to hang anything on the lines to attract them. And the fish bit so readily there was no need for reserves. Fresh water fell faster than he could use it up and a few minutes of bailing topped off the water tank.

He missed the work. Fishing and keeping his knife and tackle free of rust still helped the mornings pass, and at night there were the birds and sleep. But the afternoons were interminable.

Legs drawn up so that his chin rested on his knees, he sat, chewing his lips, tugging at his beard and hair, staring out at sea and sky. There were village watches whose jobs were to guard the crops from bandits. Day after day, night after night, they squatted in front of their little straw huts, staring across watery fields green with rice, ever alert for a ripple, the slightest noise that warned of possible trespass. Lim, his senses equally sharp, also looked for and noticed the least change: a luminescent slick glimmering in the moonlight; a cloud of insects that strode on the surface of the sea as easily as the little night birds; a swarm of tiny crabs and shrimps. But the intruders he hoped for did not come. And when he plucked the half-rotted carcass of a dead bird out of the sea, he wondered if someday, someone might do the same to him.

Lying dry and warm between the covers of his canvas bedding, Lim watched spokes of light rise from far below the horizon. Bright as searchlight beams, they caught a smudge not much larger than a mote of dust in their pink glow. Was it one of the birds that came at night and left with the dawn, or a new daytime bird on its way to his larder for the first time? The tiny silhouette vanished into darkness, reappeared in the next spear of light, then vanished entirely as the rosy beams spread and fused, turning all the eastern sky and sea an ox-blood red. Almost immediately, the sun burst above the distant hills of swells, and the red turned orange, then sizzled into a fiery copper that burned off the predawn chill, signalling Lim to begin his daily routine.

He spread his bedding out to dry, leaned over the side

of the raft to wash the sleep out of his eyes, noticed the water held a reddish tinge though he faced west. Puzzled, he glanced up at the sky. There was no trace of red anywhere in the diffuse gold. He scanned the sea on all sides, beginning with the area closest to the raft. The coloration, faint yet distinct, spread as far as he could see, and a cluster of debris glinted on the surface. The wreck of a ship?

Lim's pulse quickened. There might be people out there, a submarine lurking below, rescue on its way. He dipped his right hand into the sea and played with the water. Thinking back to the day the *Benlomond* was torpedoed, he remembered the huge slicks of black oil that had covered the water. Was this snag of debris from an old wreck then? Or could this strange pinkish color be a dye dropped by a plane to mark the wreckage? He withdrew his hand and rubbed it across his thigh and belly. His skin, dark brown and streaked with grime, shone wetly for a moment. Then the moisture evaporated, leaving no stain.

On an impulse, he cast the fishing line with the large hook, aiming at the dark clump floating a few yards distant. His first attempt fell short; the second failed to catch hold of anything substantial; and the third time, the hook snagged, falling off as he pulled in the line. Squinting, he gauged the distance and the effect the morning breeze might have, then cast again.

The hook, sinking in the middle of the debris, resisted when he tugged. Feeling the weight against the line, Lim grinned, knowing the hook had caught. But the smile quickly faded as the line pulled taut and he realized he might lose the hook. Swiftly he payed the line out. Then, careful not to cause any undue pressure, he brought up the slack and dragged in the line.

It was a tree trunk, he realized, not wreckage, and his heart raced as he pulled it close and heaved it on board. The mass of barnacles and the degree of decay indicated the trunk had floated at sea perhaps as long as he had. But he could not stop the surge of fresh hope as he dipped a tin into the sea, the exultation when the water settled, leaving a brown film at the bottom of the tin. Silt. He was close to a river. Land.

By late afternoon, the color of the sea had deepened into a muddy brown. He saw more clumps of driftwood, fished out a string of seaweed with tough little berries that tasted of salt. Studying the horizon, he thought the dark line beneath a bank of clouds might be land. But intermittent showers and then darkness obliterated it before he could be sure.

Too excited to sleep, he peered into the moonlit night. The rain had cleared the air and the stars sparkled. Phosphorescence twinkled in the earthly sea and the Heavenly River separating the Cowherd and the Weaving Maid, and Lim felt a rush of yearning for his betrothed, his parents, home.

When he finally dozed, he dreamed of the village, the dream so familiar and real he was startled to find himself still adrift when he woke. A soft breeze stirred the velvet air, kindling the embers of yesterday's sun, and small flames licked the eastern horizon, creating a rosy glow that shredded the clouds hiding the landfall he knew was there. Unable to contain himself, he shook his fists at the sky, urging the fiery streaks to hurry.

Finally, the last bits of cloud vanished, revealing a strip of solid gold: a long, low sandy beach. He crouched, staring. His muscles cramped. His eyeballs burned, blurring the stretch of gold. But he dared not move lest it disappear.

Dark smudges like the ones he had seen the morning before passed above. He counted three, realized they were not birds as he had guessed, but planes. A coastal patrol? The pilots would never distinguish the brown raft and grubby gray canopy from the muddy water. But the pilot that had dropped the dye had noticed the flag, and it was still relatively white and clean. Heart pounding, Lim leaped into the well, dug out the flag, leaned over the side and waved it though the planes were gliding straight across the far horizon just above the golden band.

The last plane disappeared.

The sun rose and the stretch of beach became lost in the glitter of ocean and sky.

But it seemed to Lim that his catch had the look and taste of freshwater fish and the swell no longer followed the regular pattern of the open sea, that he could hear breakers pounding against a shore and smell trees, grass, and earth.

Driftwood, tree bark, a piece of cork knocked against the raft. And just before dusk, he drifted into an uprooted tree with leaves still green. Everything pointed to land. But the sandy beach remained as distant as Peng'lai, the mythical islands that floated freely, without anchor, drifting close enough for men to hear their siren call, see their glittering sands, and smell and taste the fragrance of their magical herbs, but never close enough to touch.

Among the birds that came that night was a land bird that had no webs between its claws and Lim stalked it with his eyes, for whichever direction the bird flew, there would be land. But the bird, perched on a string between the poles, showed no desire to leave.

Lim's calves ached from squatting. Yet much as he wanted the bird to fly away, he dared not frighten it by moving in case that brought him bad luck. Finally, the bird swooped down onto the deck. Scarcely daring to breathe, Lim's eyes tracked it as it hopped across the planks, pecking here and there, then took off, its wings beating rapidly. He wheeled around to follow the bird's flight — saw the moon etched with delicate black markings. Branches.

Motionless and flat as a paper cut-out, the branches and moon looked unreal. He closed his eyes, opened them. The dark silhouette in front of the yellow quarter moon was still there. Deliberately, he turned his back on it and paced the deck, eyes down, stamping out his excitement, his desire to believe, his fear that he would be disappointed yet again.

He stopped and looked up. The moon had risen above the lacy network of black branches, but he could see the ragged silhouette of tree tops beneath its glow. He knelt, leaned over the side and scooped up a little water in his cupped palms, tasted it. Sweet. He must be close to the mouth of the river!

All his senses tingled with anticipation. Yet, strangely, his thoughts were of the first time he had seen the sea, and the sensations he had experienced then washed over him. The unique sea smell. The crashing sound of breakers. The glitter of waves dancing under the sun. The salty, bitter taste of the water. The feel of spindrift blowing across his face....

Morning mist blanketed the dawn, swirling like smoke from cooking fires, while under him, the raft heaved on a long coastal swell. Where had he drifted to? Was the country friendly? He had been a castaway for more than four moons. Was the war over? Who had won? Straining for a glimpse of houses and people, Lim smelled wet earth, leaves, blossoms unseen, an unfamiliar musty odor, burning wood. Visions of roast pork appeared. Steaming bowls of rice and vegetables and tea. Cool, juicy fruits. All the foods and cigarettes that would be spread before him within the day, hours, minutes.

As the gentle morning breeze tore jagged windows in

the drenching mists, he saw the tips of lush green trees, swaying fronds of palms. Gradually the steamy tendrils scattered, revealing a solid wall of black green jungle.

Stunned, Lim struggled to reassure himself. But all that came to mind was his mother scolding him when he had gone into the dense forests near their village on a boy's dare. Savages lived there, she warned. Tribesmen more than six feet tall with long hair bundled into big knots on their foreheads, warriors who hunted little boys with poison arrows and flintlock guns, kidnapping them for their women who were blue with tattoos and just as fierce as the men.

His teacher insisted that the Li people, while primitive, were friendly, so hospitable they would share their shelter and meat with strangers. Lim wanted to believe him and the lone Hakka traders who came through the village with similar assurances; to hope that if savages did live in these jungles, they would be generous and kind. But even if they were not, he did not want to drift away from the land, for as long as he hugged the coast, there was always the chance of rescue from patrol planes or boats, a clearing in the jungle that would reveal a seaport, a city, a town.

Unable to determine his course, he could only monitor the distance between raft and shore in an agony of worry as wind and current pushed the raft closer, then farther away....

There were two forests, one on top of the other. Tall trees towered forty feet above the roof of the one underneath, and mossy shrouds draped branches, while vines trailed everywhere, hanging like ropes, wrapped around tree trunks, snarled in thick underbrush. When the raft drifted close, he could hear the screech of birds, the harsh roar of animals, smell the forest, moist and heavy. Trees, grasses, vines and brush torn from the banks floated between the raft and shore, the mass of logs and debris as dangerous to the raft as mines to a ship.

Mines. Near coasts, the *Benlomond* had traveled in convoys headed by minesweepers. He was less than a mile from the shore. Might he strike a mine? Could the force of the raft set it off?

Lim eyed the water between him and the shore. Was it possible to ride in on the backs of small waves, using his broken oar to push aside debris?

He pushed away a log with the end of the oar. Tiny fish, camouflaged as leaves, flipped and swam away, vanishing in whirls of ocher water. A gnat buzzed out of the disturbance.

Slapping his thigh to kill it, Lim was reminded again of how the boys' taunts had sent him squirming through the tangle of shrubs and bamboo and saplings, how his father had found him weeping, his face and arms red and swollen from insect bites, his clothes and feet torn to shreds by long thorns and rattan vines that bristled with sharp hooks.

Even if he found an open patch where he could land safely, how could he hack a path through the jungle with a pemmican tin knife? How could he walk there on bare feet? How would he trap and kill his food? How would he defend himself from the snakes and tigers and savages that lived in jungles like these? He set down the oar. He would take his chances with the mines.

There was no break in the densely forested banks. But the water was too muddy and tasted too fresh for there not to be a river mouth somewhere and he comforted himself with images of the channel to the port in Thailand. It was so narrow that it was invisible from the sea. But at the end of it, there was a port. A city with people. And there had to be one here too. After all, the planes he had seen must have come from somewhere.

All through the long day he searched for smoke, a break in the green. With afternoon, the land sounds ceased. Then rain poured down so heavily he could not see beyond the raft, and he fretted that it might turn into a squall that would blow him away from the land or smash him ashore. Or that the land was already gone. But when the rain stopped, the jungle came alive with noise again, and with dark came a beating, insistent rhythm punctuated by shrieks, an occasional howl....

CHAPTER TWENTY-EIGHT

In his village, in Hong Kong, and among the Chinese crew, land commanded the respect of all. For land could endure droughts, floods, bandits, greedy landlords and government officials, fire or disease, and as long as there was land, there would always be hope of recovery and dreams of wealth. That was why land was coveted as well as respected. For land was perpetual. It meant safety.

Since he had become a castaway, Lim had also believed landfall would mean release from the raft, the sea. But the jungle he had drifted within sight of for the past two days offered as little relief as the sea had given when Heaven had withheld rain, and he felt as frustrated and cheated as he had then. Yet he dreaded the possibility that he might lose sight of land again. And that night, when a sudden turn of wind sent the awning billowing into a sail that pushed the raft away from shore, he slashed the ties that bound the lower corners of the awning to the corner poles.

The wind or the current might still take him back out to sea, but with the moon hidden behind clouds, he could not see, and in the morning, low clouds shrouded the raft. Agonizingly slowly they dissolved, the filmy threads fanning out like phoenix tails, revealing blue green islands rising out of an amber sea. A fleet of fishing boats.

Swathed in mists and a haze of water vapor, the boats seemed unreal, and Lim trembled as he waved and shouted, his voice ghostly as the shadowy sails.

He shook the canvas awning up and down, swung it sideways. The activity gave him courage, and he shouted with more conviction. "Help me! Help!"

He was hoarse long before the haze burned off enough for him to see clearly. Yet so long as there was the slightest chance the fishermen were real, he could not stop.

The maze of swampy, low-lying islands grew clearer. But if there had been a fleet of boats, they were gone. Except one.

Thirty feet long, with a little cabin and a single brown sail, it looked like a junk, and Lim wondered, with a sudden leap of his heart, if he had by some miracle drifted back to Hainan, since all seas were connected.

Though the boat seemed to be sailing towards him, he could not be sure that he had been seen. But when he opened his mouth to shout, there was only a small, hoarse rattle. He cracked the canvas awning hard against the deck. The sound echoed across the water like pistol shots and he stopped, afraid his intentions might be mistaken, waved the white flag of surrender instead.

"Help!" he croaked in Chinese, then English. "Help!"

Closer now, he saw that the sail was well patched and the boat not much more than crudely carved-out logs lashed together. Were the people on it savages? He stopped waving. Straining, he made out three figures on the deck. A man. A woman. A girl. They were dark, too dark to be Chinese, and their clothing seemed Western.

The man waved.

He had been seen! Quickly Lim held the white flag high.

"English?" the man called.

Lim froze, not knowing how to answer. He thought of the ship's master who had examined him, felt the piercing glint of the binoculars, the ship turning away. His belly knotted, the pain a pale echo of far greater hurts.

"English?" the man shouted again.

Lim plowed his fingers through his tangle of hair and beard. Should he pretend to be English since the man expected it? Would the man help him if he admitted he was not?

Slowly Lim shook his head. "Chinese." He waved the flag with one hand, pointed at himself with the other. "Chinese," he repeated. "Me Chinese."

Suddenly he was aware of his nakedness. Embarrassed, he lowered the flag, holding it like a shield before him, uncertain what he should do or say next.

The man turned to the woman who disappeared below. To tell the person steering the boat to turn? But the boat did not turn, and the woman came back up on deck and walked sure-footed to the stern.

The tapered prow cut through the water, nosing closer despite a drop in the wind. Within inches of crashing into the raft, it swerved expertly, and the woman at the stern grabbed one of the raft's corner poles, while from the prow, the man pitched a coil of rope at Lim. He caught it easily and looped it around a pole. The boat pulled up alongside, and the man, smiling, held out his hand to help Lim on board.

He was sure the man meant him no harm. Yet he hesitated, feeling an unexpected reluctance to leave, the raft suddenly secure, while the boat, the people and the jungle were unknown. Slowly, he gathered the knife and fishing tackle he had depended on for so long.

The man gestured, asking if Lim wanted the raft towed, and though he knew it was foolish, Lim felt a fleeting temptation to nod yes as he took the man's hand and climbed on board the fishing boat.

But he pushed the raft away, shaking his head, "No."

EPILOGUE

The Brazilian fishing family picked Poon Lim up ten miles off the coast of Brazil, east of Salinas, in the State of Para. He sailed with them for three days before they landed at Belém. Instead of the foods he had dreamed of, Poon's first meals were farinha and cooked fish. The fishermen did have tobacco, however, and according to the "British Intelligence Report," Poon "was overjoyed and sang and laughed and ate voraciously."

Two months earlier, three seamen from the *S.S. Zaandam* (a Dutch luxury liner leased by the United States) were rescued from a raft not far from where the fishermen found Poon. Adrift for 83 days, the men were emaciated and close to death, and they had to be carried on board the American minesweeper that found them. When the Brazilian fishermen brought Poon to Belém on April 6, 1943, he had been a castaway for 133 days, a record which remains unbroken to this day. Nevertheless, he walked ashore unassisted.

The British Consul, amazed at Poon's physical condition, took him to a photographer before checking him into the Beneficência Portuguesa Hospital in Belém. And *Estado do Pará*, the local newspaper, reported that Poon, though "burned black . . . does not at all show signs of the 133 days of hunger and thirst and fight against the waves, the sun and the weather."

Thirty pounds underweight, Poon's only complaint was of "stomach disturbances," and a belief that he had worms. The hospital doctor found no indication of worms, only a "derangement of the stomach, probably due to the raw food which he had eaten for so long and to exposure."[1]

Four months later, Poon still had little or no appetite and would only drink milk. According to American doctors, "Similar manifestations occur in the stories of other survivors and may be one of the characteristics of a mild neurosis resulting from the strain of sea survival experience."[2]

Poon was discharged after forty-five days of rest and observation in the Beneficência Portuguesa Hospital, "where the nuns, who did not at first like the idea of taking charge of a Chinese, all became delighted with him."[3] The British Consul and The Ben Line arranged for Poon to fly to Miami on an army plane and then take a train to New York, where he could wait for transport to England.

Interviewing survivors was standard wartime practice, and while Poon was in Miami, he was questioned by the U.S. Navy. According to the report, "Details before and after the attack are very vague, the reason being that the only survivor is a Chinaman [*sic*] who was 2nd Steward on the boat, and who has only a limited knowledge of English."[4] The report further concluded "Survivor's description of the flag indicates sub was Italian." All subsequent American reports and articles repeated this assumption as fact.

Had the U.S. Navy Lieutenant who interviewed Poon checked with Britain's Ministry of Defense or Lloyd's, he would have discovered that the *Benlomond* was sunk by the German U-172 commanded by D. Carl Emmermann.[5] In correspondence with the author, Emmermann confirmed that the white and green Poon saw on the submarine's conning tower were the colors of the U-172's insignia, a white Neptune on a green sea. And the submarine's log for November 23, 1942, reads:

> At 0815 on 23 November the U-172 came upon a steamer at dawn, a fine angle on the bow, just below the horizon. The submarine shifted to the south staying just in sight. The steamer moved at 13 sea miles and zigzagged every 10 minutes.
>
> Submarine stalked the steamer slowly above water. At 1334 gave alarm and submerged. Observed steamer's progress. At 1410 fired a double salvo from tubes I and II. The first ran 20 seconds (400 meters); a powerful explosion followed by another, probably a boiler explosion which created a good deal of steam. The second hit came after 22 seconds (440 meters) which created another explosion in the fantail. The ship sank deeper in the stern and, after two minutes, went down stern first. Approximately 10 survivors appeared on a raft.
>
> At 1415 surfaced and discovered that it was the *Benlomond*. . . .
>
> U-172 departed at 1444 for a new operational area.[6]

Despite the dismissive attitude conveyed in the U.S. Navy's Intelligence report, Poon's achievement caught the attention of Lieutenant Samuel Harby, who arranged to have Poon interviewed through interpreters at the Navy's Emergency Rescue Equipment Section in New York. Following Poon's specifications, the Navy constructed a duplicate raft. Poon also demonstrated how he had made his fishing tackle and knife, and the film and photographs the U.S. Navy made of his reenactment were used for recruitment and to provide valuable survival information to personnel. Ironically, when Poon tried to join the Navy, he was rejected because of flat feet.

Poon received many tributes. The British Colony in Belém presented him with a watch engraved, "To Poon Lim, bravest of the brave." He was authorized by special order of the War Shipping Administration to wear the United States Merchant Marine Combat Bar with One Star, for "His courage and fortitude will be an enduring inspiration to merchant seamen of all the United Nations."[7] King George VI invested him with the British Empire Medal for "display[ing] exceptional courage, fortitude, and resource in overcoming the tremendous difficulties with which he was faced during the long and dangerous voyage on the raft."[8] The Ben Line presented him with a watch, a pair of cuff links, and the back pay he had accrued during his 133 days on the raft. And the Executive Council of the Chinese Republican Government awarded him a Certificate of Honor.

In an interview for the *Empire News* shortly after his survival, Poon said:

> I hope that my experience will prove that the Chinese in this war can face hardships as well as the gallant seamen of other nationalities, and can come through them without losing heart.
>
> I hope that this fact will lead to the betterment of the conditions of my fellow seamen and stewards, not only during the war but after the war.
>
> The sea does not know the difference between the yellow man and the white man.
>
> On a raft one is just a human being at the mercy, to some extent, of what is to come, but dependent on one's self for wanting to carry on.
>
> And so all of us who sail in ships and face the perils of sea should have equal conditions. It is better so not only for Chinese, but for all.

Like other Chinese, however, Poon was prohibited by the 1882 Exclusion Law from immigrating to the United States. For Poon to remain in New York, the Chinese

Consul had to obtain a "temporary visitor" visa from the Immigration and Naturalization Service. Even after the repeal of the Exclusion Law (December 18, 1943), the annual quota for Chinese immigrants was 105, making a change from "temporary visitor" to permanent status virtually impossible.

Through the intervention of the Chinese Vice Consul, Poon was permitted to work as a parts inspector for the Wright Aeronautical Corporation in New Jersey during the war years and, when the war ended, as a messman for the United States Lines. Four years later, the persistent efforts of Lt. Commander Samuel Harby finally resulted in the introduction of a special bill in the 81st Congress by Senator Warren G. Magnussen "To provide for the admission to, and the permanent residence in, the United States of Poon Lim."[9] President Truman signed Private Law 178 on July 27, 1949, and the final papers for Poon's citizenship were completed in 1952.

As a U.S. citizen, Poon was not permitted to enter the People's Republic of China. Since he could not go home, he asked his parents to travel to Hong Kong to see him. The woman he had been betrothed to, believing him dead, had married someone else. But one of Poon's former shipmates from the *S.S. Tanda* matched Poon with his daughter, Chan Mei Mui. They were married on December 1, 1952, and settled in Brooklyn, New York, where they raised three daughters and a son.

Poon Lim continued to work for the United States Lines, retiring as Chief Steward in 1983, exactly forty years after his ordeal. In 1986, he and his wife visited his native village on Hainan Island, and Poon received the hero's welcome that he'd dreamed of while on the raft.

He died in Brooklyn on January 4, 1991.

1. "British Weekly Intelligence Report," November 1944.
2. "Emergency Rescue Equipment Section Survival Account No. 1, Appendix A," U.S. Navy, July 22, 1943.
3. "British Weekly Intelligence Report," November 1944.
4. "Memorandum for File," U.S. Navy Dept., Office of the Chief Naval Operations, May 27, 1943.
5. "British Naval Intelligence Documents," October– December 1942, vol. 15; Lloyd's World War II Loss Books.
6. Log for U-172, November 23, 1942, translated by Charles Burdick.
7. Letter by E. S. Land, War Shipping Administration, Washington, D.C.
8. *The London Gazette*, July 13, 1943.
9. U.S., Congress, Senate, S. Res. 1405, 81st Congress, March 25 (legislative day, March 18) 1949.

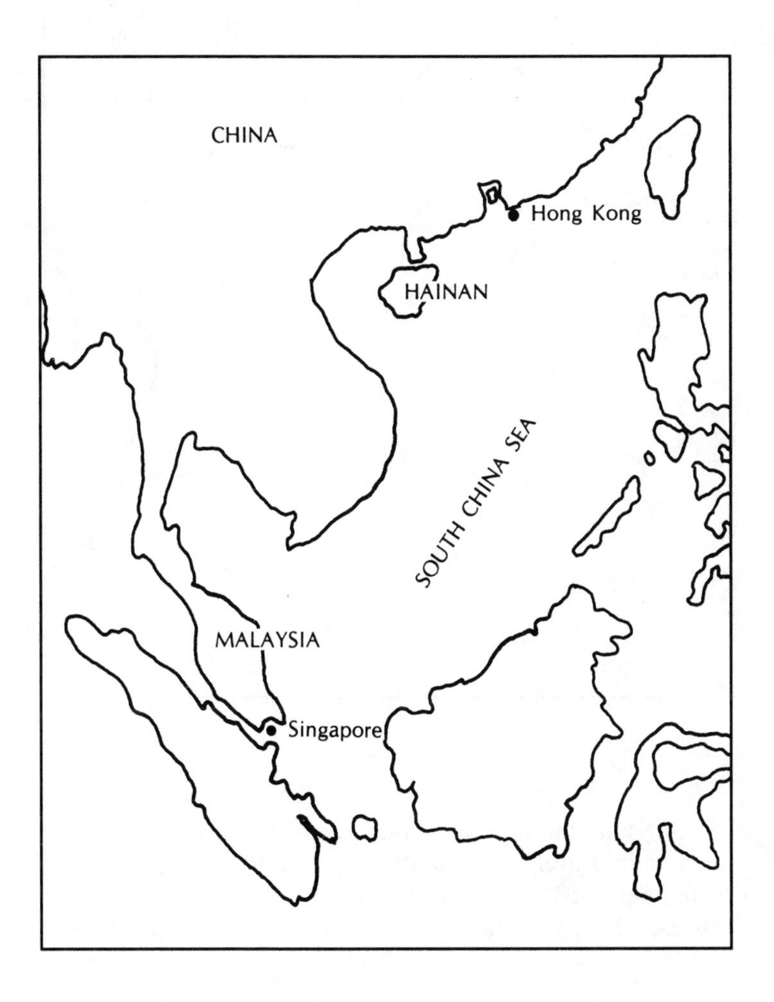

Though rich in resources, Hainan's people have traditionally been impoverished, forcing villagers like Poon Lim and his brother to seek work in Hong Kong and Malaya (now Malaysia).

The Benlomond was sailing from Capetown to Paramaribo in Dutch Guiana (now Surinam) when she was torpedoed. 133 days later, Poon Lim was picked up at the mouth of the Amazon River by fishermen who took him to Belém.

Poon Lim an hour after landing in Belém, Brazil.
(*Courtesy of Poon Lim*)

The Brazilian fishing family that picked Poon up gave him the clothes he is wearing in this picture.

"A comparison of Poon Lim's photograph . . . with those taken of other great survivors on rescue shows a decided difference, favorable to him. . . .

"(His) experience is a wonderful example of how a rugged physique and resourcefulness of mind will extend the limits of human endurance beyond all expectations." ("They Survived at Sea," Lt. Comdr. Samuel F. Harby, *National Geographic*, May 1945)

(Courtesy of Poon Lim)

After the interviews, the U.S. Navy asked Poon to reenact his experiences on the raft. The Emergency Rescue Equipment Section constructed a raft following the specifications in a model Poon made, then added the yellow distress flag which is lashed to one of the poles. The poles are also slightly shorter and less sturdy than the original, and a make-up artist provided Poon with the false beard and clothes.

The photograph was taken in New York harbor, site of the reenactment.

During the reenactment, Poon demonstrated how he made his tools and fished.

(*Courtesy of Poon Lim*)

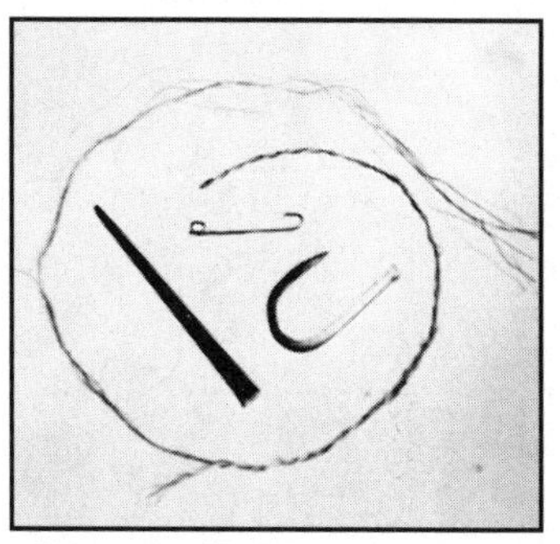

(*Courtesy of Poon Lim*)

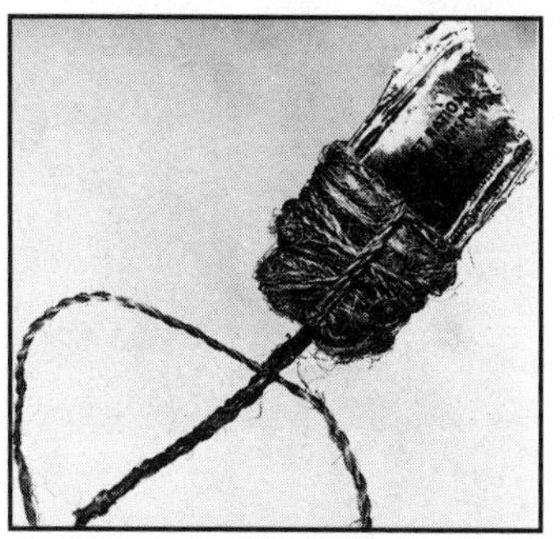

(*Courtesy of Poon Lim*)

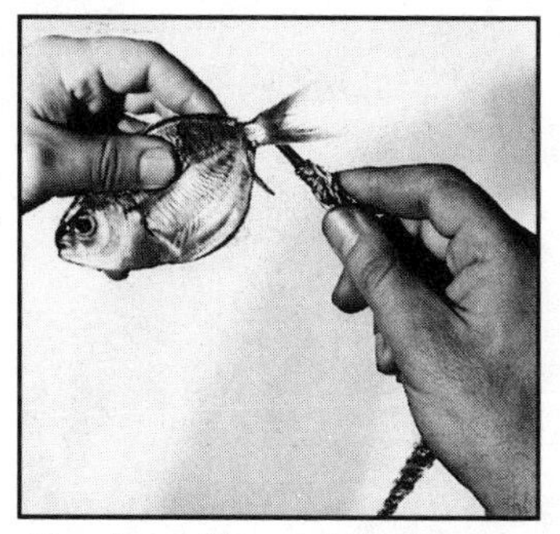

(*Courtesy of Samuel Harby and National Geographic*)

1. Braiding a fishing line.

2. Part of the fishing line, a ship's nail, a ship's nail transformed into a hook, and a hook mde out of the spring from a flashlight.

3. A knife made from a pemmican tin lid.

4. Hooking a small fish so that it could still swim and attract a larger fish.

AUTHOR'S NOTE

I based *Sole Survivor* on interviews with Poon Lim, his wife, and his brother Gee Han, as well as newspaper and magazine articles, American and British Intelligence Reports, The Ben Line histories, and additional research. Although I made every attempt to maintain accuracy, the reader should take the following into consideration.

At the time of his rescue, Poon Lim had a very limited knowledge of Cantonese and English. None of the persons who interviewed him then, including the interpreters, spoke the Hainan dialect, which was Mr. Poon's native language. As a result there are many discrepancies in the various articles and reports. Some of these inaccuracies have been repeated until they have become "fact," and it is now impossible to discover the original truth.

My own interviews with Mr. Poon were conducted in Cantonese and English. While his vocabulary in both languages had expanded considerably since 1943, the Hainan dialect continued to be the language in which he was the most proficient.

Our first interview took place in February 1982. Though Mr. Poon's memory of his 133 days on the raft was excellent, his accounts were filtered through forty years of additional experiences. His memories were also recounted in the knowledge that they would become a book, his legacy for his children and grandchildren.

Because I chose to write the book in the style of a novel, the first edition of *Sole Survivor* was published as fiction. Fourteen years later, the use of fiction techniques in writing nonfiction is no longer unusual. Hence *Sole Survivor* is being reissued as nonfiction.